THE VISIBLE EXPERT®

REVOLUTION

HOW TO TURN ORDINARY EXPERTS INTO THOUGHT LEADERS, RAINMAKERS AND INDUSTRY SUPERSTARS

"*The Visible Expert® Revolution* is a great read for any expert—
whether you are relatively well known already or want to make
your mark for the first time. You will learn not only what's inhibiting
your growth, but also specific strategies, techniques and advice
to overcome self-doubt, increase your visibility and build your
reputation. If you are an expert, this is the guide you've been
waiting for!"

> » **CHRIS MERCER**, Valuation Expert, Author of *Business Valuation:*
> *An Integrated Theory, Unlocking Private Company Wealth, Buy-Sell*
> *Agreements for Baby Boomer Business Owners,* Founder and
> Chairman of Mercer Capital

"If you want to stand out in your field, this book will show you
how to accelerate your journey. Chock full of research, practical
examples and actions you can take, it's essential reading. Put it
at the top of your list!"

> » **TOM HOOD, BCPA, CGMA, CITP**, EVP Business Engagement & Growth
> at the Association of International Certified Professional Accountants
> (AICPA)

"An amazingly useful guide to help position yourself (and your
company) as the go-to resource. Provides a truly helpful strategic/
how-to combination for experts at any stage of the journey."

> » **JOE PULIZZI**, Author, *Epic Content Marketing* and *Content Inc.*

The Visible Expert Revolution: How to Turn Ordinary Experts into Thought Leaders, Rainmakers and Industry Superstars

Published by the Hinge Research Institute
1851 Alexander Bell Drive, Suite 350
Reston, Virginia 20191

ISBN 978-0-9904459-4-4

Visit our website at **www.hingemarketing.com**

CONTENTS

...SOME FIRMS STILL DON'T REALIZE THE MARKET HAS UNDERGONE A REVOLUTION. AND IF THEY DON'T ADAPT TO THESE CHANGES SOON, THEIR PROSPECTS FOR SUCCESS WILL FADE AWAY.

INTRODUCTION

THE OLD REGIME IS COLLAPSING. Many of the traditional pillars of professional services marketing that supported business development success year after year after year lie toppled, broken and neglected in the marketplace of expertise. Today's buyers of professional services have their own ideas about how to find, evaluate and select a firm to solve their business problems. With modern tools and a new way of seeing the world shaped by the internet, these young upstarts have pulled off a coup, and many firms are still asking themselves, "What happened?" Even now, some firms still don't realize the market has undergone a revolution. And if they don't adapt to these changes soon, their prospects for success will fade away.

While the king of professional services marketing—the word-of-mouth referral—may not be dead or even deposed, it has lost its supremacy. And many of its peers, such as sponsorships, networking events and tradeshows, deliver less impact than before. That's because so many buyers have moved online where they are no longer engaged in those activities. In the new world order of professional services marketing, a new movement is replacing the old. We call this movement the rise of the Visible Expert®.

If you've ever listened to a keynote speaker at a conference, followed a leader in your industry online or read an influential book about your area of expertise, you have experienced firsthand the power of a Visible Expert. These are the authorities in their fields who stand a little taller and whose words carry more weight. The media seeks them out for quotes, and businesses are happy to pay a premium for their thinking. What separates a Visible Expert from an ordinary expert? It's not necessarily superior intellect or charisma. The vast majority of Visible Experts we interviewed over the past fifteen years are regular people who, like you, have faced challenges, setbacks and self-doubt during their careers. What sets these high profile individuals apart is their command of the marketplace of ideas. But they didn't get there by accident. They took that high ground deliberately, in small incremental steps.

With a little revolutionary thinking, you can do the same.

WHO IS THIS BOOK FOR?

Whether you are a solo practitioner or part of a professional services firm, this book will show you how to achieve extraordinary success.

Are you an individual expert who wants to raise your professional profile, speak with greater authority and command higher fees? In these pages, you will find a clear, proven roadmap to elevate your visibility and prestige with less frustration—*and up to five times faster*—than if you tried to figure it out on your own. This book will explain how to draw up your own visibility plan, including a customized, research-based strategy and a detailed implementation calendar. Along the way, we will provide you detailed instructions, as well as advice from nine real-world Visible Experts from the accounting, AEC, consulting, legal and government contracting industries. And at each step, we provide detailed examples you can use as models as you create your own roadmap.

As you read the stories of the real-life Visible Experts in these pages, you may notice that some are individual experts with firms of their own. As the public face of their firms, they rely on their colleagues to help them build their visibility. This situation isn't uncommon. As individual experts begin to achieve visibility and demand for their services, they often hire people to support their growing business. Other solo practitioners prefer the flexibility and low overhead of going it alone. Still others, of course, work in large organizations.

This book is also for professional services firms—organizations that want to take one or many of their experts through a structured process to make them more visible and valuable. As you will learn later, a Visible Expert's luster can rub off onto their firm, raising the fortunes of the entire organization. You will meet an attorney who has built an entire firm of Visible Experts—and upon that foundation an enviable global reputation. If you own, manage or market a professional services firm, this book will show you how you can put together a repeatable program to raise your experts to prominence. Unlike individuals who have to tackle everything themselves, firms often have a range of specialized skills and resources they can call on to support their Visible Experts. This support can take much of the burden off of the individual practitioners and dramatically accelerate their progress.

Now, this book isn't for everyone. First, if you are not yet a bona fide expert, we can't teach you your craft.* You have to bring some game to the game, and you can't use the approach in this book to fake your way to fame. Second, If you don't believe in sharing your expertise, you are going to struggle to achieve success. That said, this program is not about overt self-promotion, either. The Visible Experts we researched didn't get where they are because they are prima donnas. Rather, they built their reputations upon trust and goodwill, which they earned gradually over time by freely giving away advice and samples of their expertise—and telling their audiences where to find more of their insights. They succeed not because they are great at selling themselves but because they are great at teaching and sharing.

ABOUT THE RESEARCH

This book is the product of fifteen years of interviews with hundreds of Visible Experts across almost every professional services industry. Our first book on the topic, *The Visible Expert,* introduced the concept to the world and described the benefits of becoming a high-profile expert. Since its publication, we've learned even more about the paths professionals take to pre-eminence. And we've learned a great deal about what worked and where they took unproductive wrong turns. We have also taken dozens of individuals

---

* We can, however, teach you some tricks to keep your expertise razor sharp—see Chapter 7.

and firms through our Visible Expert program—where we were able to witness professionals' journeys firsthand and refine the process. The program and advice we lay out in this book is the culmination of this research and experiences.

WHY WE WROTE THIS BOOK

How did we get interested in Visible Experts in the first place? Our firm, Hinge, specializes in helping professional services firms grow faster and build more engaging brands. But that meant we needed to understand the dynamics that drive superior marketing. In 2008, we launched the Hinge Research Institute to study how firms marketed themselves, as well as how the people who bought their services behaved. We paid special attention to that subset of organizations that grew faster and were more profitable, year after year. We noticed that these firms began to market themselves differently. More and more, they were leading with their expertise. They were enlisting their experts to deliver a steady stream of high-quality content, which seemed to benefit all parties.

At the same time, we noticed that buyers were changing. As a younger generation rose into management roles they brought a new set of habits and expectations to their businesses. Barely able to remember a world without the internet, these young professionals assumed that information was free and available anytime they wanted it. They also were raised in a retail environment in which people routinely found, evaluated and bought products online. The convergence of these two habits sparked a revolution. One that is still playing out today.

These insights led us to think about the experts who had risen to the top of their fields. We had so many questions. What made them special? Where did these stars fit into the new marketplace of knowledge? How did they achieve their elite status? What about ordinary experts? Was there a path they could follow to elevate their visibility and improve their business prospects? To find answers we began conducting more research, including interviewing scores of leading industry experts to hear their stories and, we hoped, uncover a road that others could follow. The rest, as they say, is... well, in this book!

CHAPTER ONE

WHY BECOME A VISIBLE EXPERT?

YOU MAY NOT ENCOUNTER UNRULY CROWDS, BURNING TIRES OR BARRICADES IN THE STREETS, BUT A REVOLUTION IS QUIETLY AND IRREPRESSIBLY RESHAPING THE PROFESSIONAL SERVICES. This revolution is driven by three profound changes in the marketplace.

First, over the past decade, buyer behavior has changed in fundamental ways. The tools and techniques buyers use to find, evaluate and select service providers are very different from those buyers used ten years ago. As a result, the traditional ways professional services firms reached new prospects and persuaded them to buy have been turned on their head. Even Old Faithful itself, the word-of-mouth referral, has been in steady decline for years.

Second, fast-evolving technologies—from search engines to artificial intelligence—are accelerating these new buying patterns. Today, prospective clients can seek out business insights and services anytime, anywhere.

A third change, activated by the internet and current events, has been the swift erosion of geography as an important factor in the delivery of services. In many industries, it doesn't really matter where an expert resides. Now that there is near universal access to low-cost, easy-to-use video conferencing tools, many firms no longer need to interact in person with their clients to deliver value. And since the onset of the historic COVID-19 pandemic, remote work has become commonplace, and many clients no longer expect— or even want—on-site meetings.

While these changes give firm leadership plenty to worry about, they also present an enormous opportunity. The demand for high-quality expertise has never been greater. The rapid pace of technological innovation, together with the chaos and uncertainty of the modern business world, means today's businesses can't go it alone. More and more, they rely on outside specialists to solve complex technical and operational problems so they can adapt to a market environment that keeps changing the rules.

And what about the buyer's perspective? Buyers have more access to a wide range of professional advice and talent than ever before. Modern digital tools allow them to quickly and easily locate professionals who have the precise set of skills and expertise to address their specific challenges. Today's buyers tend to be less concerned about hiring someone local than finding the firm best qualified to solve their problem. A company in San Francisco has no qualms about hiring a firm in Boston. Or Loveland, Ohio. Or New Delhi.

So what does this revolution mean for you?

In the professional services, there's never been a better time to be an expert. Today, even ordinary experts have the ability to rise to extraordinary heights and become industry stars. And in the process of elevating their own profile, they can raise the visibility and reputation of their firms, as well.

We call these individuals Visible Experts®. And they are changing the way we discover and experience expertise.

WHAT IS A VISIBLE EXPERT®?

A Visible Expert is a professional with a high level of marketplace visibility and a reputation for expertise in a specific discipline.

These are the individuals who deliver the keynotes at major conferences. The standout names in their industries, they are quoted regularly in the press and have large followings on social media. They command premium fees and land the most high-profile projects. They are the rainmakers, thought leaders and influencers that drive their industries forward. And at the very highest level, they can even break out and shape public opinion and move markets.

Do they know something that the rest of us don't?

The short answer is, no. For the most part, they just figured it out as they went, with all the mistakes, dead ends and aha moments that come with a trial-and-error approach. But what if you could learn from their mistakes, and their successes? Whether you are an individual professional or part of a firm that employs multiple experts, this book will explain not only how to become a Visible Expert, but how to do it with less effort and in much less time.

How is that possible? To uncover the answers, we spent over a decade interviewing hundreds of Visible Experts and thousands of their clients. This research gave us deep insights into the forces that are driving today's expertise revolution—and it allowed us to identify the critical steps and shortcuts to success. We have taken these insights and developed a groundbreaking approach to Visible Expertise—a path to higher visibility that almost any expert can follow.

> THE DEMAND FOR HIGH-QUALITY EXPERTISE HAS NEVER BEEN GREATER.

Over the years, we've tested and refined these techniques. We've applied them ourselves to elevate our team's professional profiles, and many of our clients use them today to great success. In the following chapters, we will describe this approach in detail, and we will share the stories of many real-world Visible Experts who have risen from relative obscurity to become leaders in their industries. But first, let's consider why we need these high-visibility experts in the first place.

WHY THE WORLD NEEDS VISIBLE EXPERTS

The pace of change in the modern world can boggle the mind. How can already-busy organizations cope with, much less succeed in, this ever-shifting business and regulatory landscape? The answer is simple. Businesses need experts. Experts who have made it their life's mission to conquer their small corner of the world.

Experts who can lead businesses through a complex problem with confidence and guide them to solutions they never would have found on our own. But even the most extraordinary experts are of little value if they are invisible. When experts make themselves easy to find they not only improve their prospects, they give businesses access to the knowledge and skill sets they need to address critical strategic, operational and technical challenges—so they, too, can thrive.

At the same time, professional services firms that invest in the visibility and credibility of their own experts also reap big benefits. Their association with these industry stars helps firms build stronger brands, generate more new business opportunities and attract top talent.

Recent research from the Hinge Research Institute describes the wealth of benefits that organizations receive from working with Visible Experts (see Figure 1.1). The average client of a Visible Expert reported an average of four specific benefits.

» Top Benefits of Working with a Visible Expert

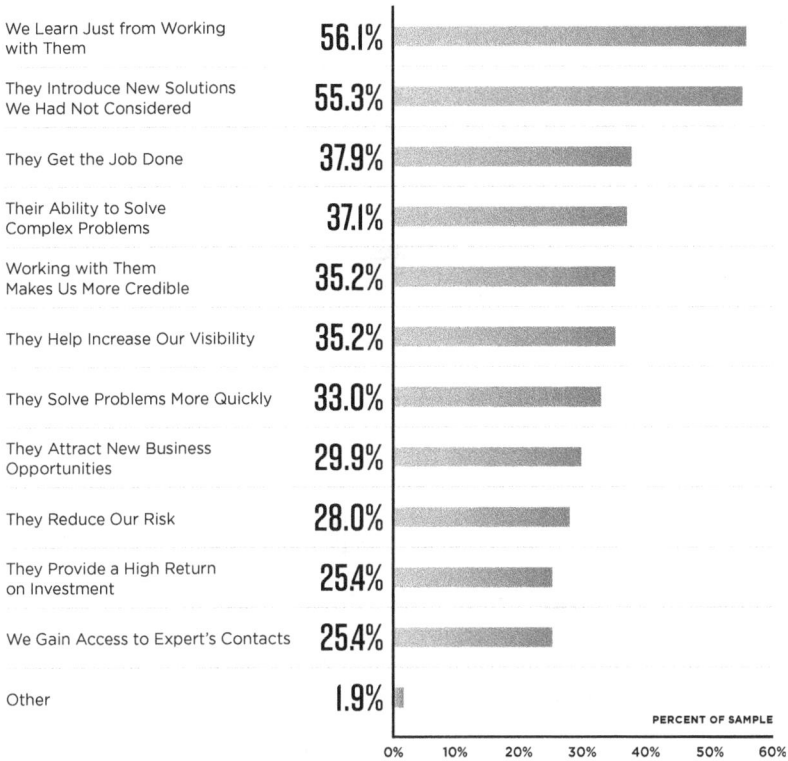

FIGURE 1.1

Benefit	Percent
We Learn Just from Working with Them	56.1%
They Introduce New Solutions We Had Not Considered	55.3%
They Get the Job Done	37.9%
Their Ability to Solve Complex Problems	37.1%
Working with Them Makes Us More Credible	35.2%
They Help Increase Our Visibility	35.2%
They Solve Problems More Quickly	33.0%
They Attract New Business Opportunities	29.9%
They Reduce Our Risk	28.0%
They Provide a High Return on Investment	25.4%
We Gain Access to Expert's Contacts	25.4%
Other	1.9%

PERCENT OF SAMPLE

0%   10%   20%   30%   40%   50%   60%

The most common benefits involve solving complex problems. No surprises there. The second most frequently cited group of benefits includes raising the visibility and credibility of the organizations that engage them. Hiring or even being associated with a Visible Expert can raise a company's credibility in the eyes of its potential clients. Many firms that are competing for large contracts will add a nationally known expert to their proposed project team to help them win the new business. For example, an architectural firm bidding on the design of an auditorium might add a Visible Expert specializing in acoustics to make its bid more appealing to the prospective client. Finally, a significant portion of clients also report that they learn and grow just from working with outside specialists.

Clearly, many factors are fueling the growing demand for Visible Experts.

WELCOME TO THE REVOLUTION

As long as there have been professions, there have been Visible Experts. Most of these experts spend much of their careers figuring out how to become widely recognized. In our early studies of high-profile experts, we noticed that these individuals fell into five levels of expertise (see Figure 1.2). These levels cover the gamut of visibility, from novice expert to international superstars like Michael Porter, Norman Foster and Bill Gates. We found that on average it took five years for an expert to advance from one level of visibility to the next. Most experts stop short of Level 5.

» The Five Levels of Visible Expertise

FIGURE 1.2

LEVEL **ONE**	**THE RESIDENT EXPERT**
	While recognized as experts by clients, staff and colleagues, these individuals are not well known outside of the firm.

LEVEL **TWO**	**THE LOCAL HERO**
	Their expert brand is becoming known beyond the boundaries of the firm, occasionally attracting new business. They are starting to engage in activities that raise their visibility, such as public speaking and blogging.

LEVEL **THREE**	**THE RISING STAR**
	Their reputation is moving onto the regional or even national stage, attracting better business and higher fees.

LEVEL **FOUR**	**THE INDUSTRY ROCK STAR**
	These experts have become nationally recognized names within their niches, driving top-tier business opportunities and commanding premium fees for themselves and their firms.

LEVEL **FIVE**	**THE GLOBAL SUPERSTAR**
	These elite experts have achieved considerable exposure outside their niches. In some cases, their names have become synonymous with their areas of expertise, and major firms clamber to be associated with them.

Today, it is possible to climb one or more levels in a single year. How? We wrote this book to explain exactly what it takes. You will learn how almost any expert—even you—can move from relative obscurity to high visibility faster than ever before.

You are going to meet a group of real-world Visible Experts who will tell their stories. Some of these experts the authors know well, as they have been long-term clients of ours. Others are luminaries we met during our many years of research into Visible Experts. Each contributes not only their experiences and perspectives, but valuable, practical lessons you can apply to your own journey.

You will meet Visible Experts who knew what they wanted to do from an early age and others who stumbled into a life-changing opportunity. You'll meet experts who had to overcome tremendous obstacles and years of hard-earned lessons, as well as a few who discovered a fast track to eminence. Along the way, you will come to realize that Visible Experts are not that different from the rest of us. Each used trial and error to find a path that led them to professional prominence.

The need for professional services expertise has never been greater, and with each new regulatory twist or technological breakthrough that demand only grows. Who benefits most from this ever-changing environment? We believe it is those experts who make the effort to become well known in their industries and are easy to find in the modern digital marketplace. Fortunately, there is now a better way to achieve these goals and seize the opportunities they create.

THREE EXPERTS. THREE PATHS.

You are about to meet three Visible Experts with very different backgrounds who have followed very different paths to achieve extraordinary recognition and professional success. You'll meet a young African-American girl from inner-city Baltimore who when she grew up climbed to the top of her profession and made history in the process. You'll meet a visionary attorney from Mumbai who defied every rule to build the most innovative law firm in Asia with an impeccable client list from around the globe. And you'll meet an architect who is on a mission to reimagine the built environment by combining two areas of expertise that to many people seem unrelated.

In their stories, you will encounter the various ways that they—and the firms they are associated with—have benefited from their Visible Expert status. More importantly, you will discover that these experts were once very much like you. They faced similar challenges and concerns. And as you meet more Visible Experts throughout this book and learn the secrets of their extraordinary success, you will come to realize that you can do it too.

Let's meet our first expert.

UNCOMMON TALENT IN UNEXPECTED PLACES

There are some moments you never forget. For Kimberly Ellison-Taylor, it was May 2015 at the Washington, DC, JW Marriott hotel. The annual meeting of the American Institute of Certified Public Accountants (AICPA), the most prestigious professional association in the field of accounting, was convening their session to select their new chairperson. Kimberly was nervous.

Earlier, two of her colleagues from the Maryland Association of CPAs had nominated her for the role of Vice-Chair, a role that automatically assumes the role of Chair the following year. But Kimberly was skeptical. "I thought I had no chance. None. At the time, we did not have the diversity we have today. I had to ask myself, are we ready for a minority chair? Not just a woman, but a black woman, married with two kids, a non-traditional background and a strong technology focus? There were so many things that could have taken me out of the running. But because my colleagues believed in me, I thought why not?"

What happened next stunned her. "When they put my name on the screen so members could vote, I turned around and everyone was standing up. There were maybe 500 or 600 people in the room, and there was a standing ovation. Everyone got to their feet and started clapping for the nomination of the Vice Chair... me! I had never experienced anything like that before."

"History was made that day," she continues. "I was almost in tears. My colleagues gave me a standing ovation because, for that moment, we all realized that the glass ceiling cracked just a little."

Kimberly is the kind of person who is easy to admire. Her intelligence, energy and character suggest that she would be successful at anything she tried. But as impressive as she and her expertise are, Kimberly has a secret weapon that amplifies the value she delivers to clients and the organizations she is associated with. It also gives her the freedom to pursue her personal passion for diversity, equity and inclusion. That secret weapon is visibility. Without visibility, expertise is often wasted.

> WITHOUT VISIBILITY, EXPERTISE IS OFTEN WASTED.

We met Kimberly Ellison-Taylor in our offices outside Washington, DC. She knows she wouldn't have been able to have an outsize impact on people were it not for her elevated status. "Being a Visible Expert offered so many advantages once I embraced it and fully understood what it meant," she said. "I grew up in the inner city of Baltimore, so I know all too well how important it is to invest in people. And I know that extraordinary things can happen to anybody. You will find uncommon talent in unexpected places. I know, because I'm an example of that."

Kimberly is not one to run from a challenge. When she found out that her preferred college did not offer an accounting major, she considered her options and what skills might help her career, whether or not she became an accountant. She came across a field called information systems. "In 1988 I didn't know that technology would become part of everything that we do, so I brought together my love of accounting and technology. But I wanted to make sure that I had the foundation to do it. When you're a Visible Expert, credentials are an important source of your credibility. So I majored in information systems management with a technical writing minor. I went on to get a master's in business administration."

But Kimberly didn't stop there. She became a licensed CPA and earned a master's degree in information technology from Carnegie Mellon University. When it comes to expertise, she is the real deal.

"As my visibility increased over the years, I've been given permission by the marketplace to become a Visible Expert in other areas, as well. For example, I didn't start out thinking about diversity, equity and inclusion. My interest in it developed through my focus on change management," she says. And Kimberly is not the only expert whose area of expertise has evolved. One of the key benefits of being a Visible Expert is the freedom it gives you to follow your interests and find new ways to make a difference in the world.

A FIRM OF VISIBLE EXPERTS
What if you had an entire firm of Visible Experts? How strong would your brand be? What could you accomplish? Few people understand the brand-building power of Visible Experts better than our next Visible Expert, Nishith Desai.

Trained as an international tax attorney, he decided to start a solo practice in his native Mumbai, India. Before long, his hard work and detailed research began to pay off. He was receiving attention for his ability to find fresh solutions to complex legal issues, especially the way the law affects multinational companies that want to do business in India. But that was only the beginning of the story. "It was in 1986," said Nishith. "My friend was the Managing Director of Bear Stearns, a famous investment banking firm which no longer exists. He suggested that I set up a law firm. I'm a barrister, and we do not usually form law firms. So I was a bit reluctant.

"I realized that one benefit of setting up a firm is you have the opportunity to train others. I was interested in developing the next generation of lawyers. That was one of the major things on my mind. But then I thought, there are hundreds of law firms on the street. How will I compete? I had no idea." A major barrier stood in his way.

What Nishith did next changed the course of his career. He conducted some research. Nishith interviewed almost 100 managing partners and senior executives at a wide range of professional services firms. He wanted to understand how they operated and thought. It was a four-year journey. He began to realize that he could not compete with established firms on their terms. They had many decades of past experience, a deep bench of talent and far greater brand recognition. He would have to find another way to compete. "Most of these firms had a hundred years or more of experience behind them," recalled Nishith. "I'm the new kid on the block, so what do I do? I thought very deeply about how to differentiate my practice.

"Little by little, a philosophy began to develop. Every new technology, every new business model, every new social, political or economic development creates a new strategic legal, tax or ethical issue. I was a researcher, as well as a lawyer. So I began to look at new technologies and forecast trends. I tried to look three, five, even fifteen years out and start preparing for that place—so when the time came, I would be ready to meet those challenges."

Eventually, Nishith decided to compete on specialized expertise. He would do this by studying emerging issues, especially those where technology and social change meet the law. Today, these issues include legally unsettled areas such as artificial intelligence, biotechnology, blockchain technology, autonomous vehicles and drones.

But specialized expertise alone was not enough. "One of the biggest lessons I learned was that training and upskilling are not enough. You have to make your people visible. Visibility to the client, to the industry and to society are very important. This commitment is something that really helped me shape the firm."

The visibility that individual experts achieve also benefits the organization as a whole. According to Nishith, "If you make people visible, automatically the organization is visible."

In just a few years, Nishith Desai Associates became well known and respected in the international legal community. But its program of developing visible expertise in emerging areas of technology has only continued to grow. All attorneys in the firm are encouraged to pursue their own "micro monopolies"—areas of special focus— and share their expertise and insights with the legal community. By encouraging research, education and outreach across the organization, Nishith Desai has built an entire firm of Visible Experts.

Today, Nishith Desai Associates attracts the world's most prominent and successful multinational companies. Its sterling reputation, visibility and thought leadership also draw a surplus of talent eager to join the firm and become Visible Experts themselves. It's little wonder that *The Financial Times* consistently names Nishith Desai Associates the most innovative law firm in Asia.

How was Nishith able to turn a team of individual experts into a powerful global brand? The answer involves a powerful psychological principle called the halo effect.

In 1915, a researcher named Edward Thorndike conducted a study to learn how people judge each other. He discovered that if a person exhibited one strong positive trait—such as being attractive— it would positively influence the rater's perception of that person's other traits. A subject's intelligence or work ethic, for instance, tended to be rated equally as strong. Thorndike named this phenomenon "the halo effect." Later studies determined that the same effect applies to businesses, which explains why branding and marketing can be so persuasive.

The halo effect has tangible implications for Visible Experts and their firms, as well. If buyers have strong, positive feelings about an expert, they are likely to believe that the expert's firm is pretty wonderful, too. In this way, Visible Experts can benefit their firms in every category that counts, including growth, reputation, partnerships, fees and closing rates. Or as Nishith pointed out, making experts visible automatically makes their firm visible, too.

What about the impact of Visible Expertise on new business development? To many experts and their firms, attracting more of the best kinds of clients is their holy grail. As it turns out, that is exactly what happens. And the halo effect is only part of the story.

THE GREENEST BUILDING
Our third Visible Expert, Carl Elefante, is Architect and Principal Emeritus at Quinn Evans Architects. Early in his career, he developed an interest in sustainability. In many ways, Quinn Evans, which has a strong focus on historic preservation, was an unlikely destination for Carl. Architects interested in preserving historic places rarely thought about sustainability, and champions of green design hardly ever worked on older structures.

Carl recalls a seminal conversation with Michael Quinn, one of the firm's founders. "I talked about my notion of environmental stewardship. He talked about his idea of cultural and heritage stewardship. We both walked away from that meeting super excited about the possibilities. You could do sustainable stewardship. We kind of created a new market, a new brand, a new product of sustainable stewardship. And the marketplace 'got' it."

Carl had ambitions of becoming a thought leader, which took a giant leap forward when he coined the phrase, "The greenest building is one that is already built." In 2018, he was elected president of the American Institute of Architects, a pinnacle of prestige in the industry.

Carl is quick to acknowledge the contributions of his talented colleagues to his success. But he also recognizes the power of having Visible Experts at Quinn Evans. "I think there are two key benefits to the firm. The first is new projects. It literally helps us get work. The second is that it helps us understand who we are and the value we bring to the table. That projects to the people in the room. They feel it. They understand that we've got the A-team here."

WHAT ARE THE BENEFITS OF BEING A VISIBLE EXPERT?

Heightened visibility offers a wide range of advantages. Figure 1.3 lists the top benefits of Visible Expertise according to the Visible Experts and their firms studied in our latest research. While personal flexibility and providing a platform for their personal message are very important rewards to some experts, the leading benefit was the way Visible Expertise boosted their brand.

FIGURE 1.3

» Top Benefits of Visible Expertise to Experts and their Firms

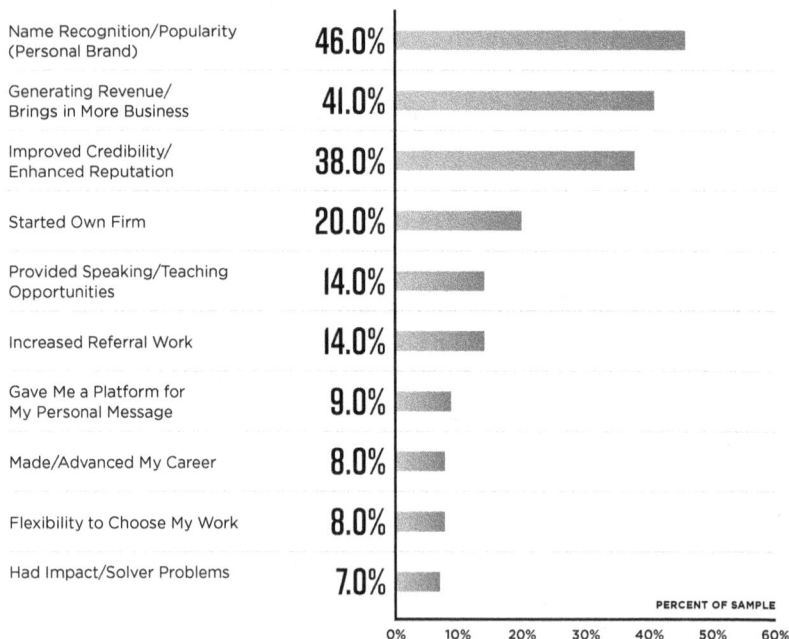

Benefit	Percent
Name Recognition/Popularity (Personal Brand)	46.0%
Generating Revenue/ Brings in More Business	41.0%
Improved Credibility/ Enhanced Reputation	38.0%
Started Own Firm	20.0%
Provided Speaking/Teaching Opportunities	14.0%
Increased Referral Work	14.0%
Gave Me a Platform for My Personal Message	9.0%
Made/Advanced My Career	8.0%
Flexibility to Choose My Work	8.0%
Had Impact/Solver Problems	7.0%

PERCENT OF SAMPLE

0%   10%   20%   30%   40%   50%   60%

WHAT DO VISIBLE EXPERTS EARN?

If there is one subject that interests most professionals and their firms, it's billing rates. So we decided to study them. We had anticipated that buyers would be willing to pay more for a Visible Expert, but we had no idea just how much more. Our research revealed that buyers are willing to pay over ten times more for a Level 5 Visible Expert than for a regular professional!

» Earning Potential by Visible Expert Level

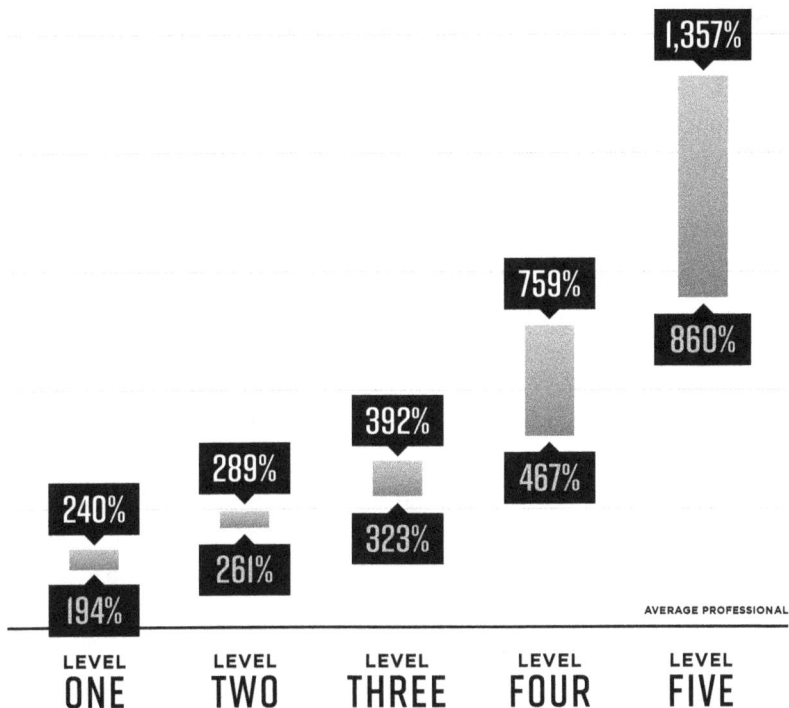

FIGURE 1.4

1,357%

759%

860%

392%

289%

467%

240%

323%

261%

194%

AVERAGE PROFESSIONAL

| LEVEL ONE | LEVEL TWO | LEVEL THREE | LEVEL FOUR | LEVEL FIVE |

In fact, Visible Experts at *every* level command premium rates, starting at about 200% of the baseline for a Level 1 Visible Expert. And as an individual's level of visibility steps upward, the rate rises dramatically. This means firms that have one or more Visible Experts on their team are able to charge the highest industry fees.

WHAT DOES IT TAKE TO BECOME A VISIBLE EXPERT?

Let's get one thing out of the way: You can't be a Visible Expert unless you are in fact an expert. You can't fake true expertise. It's the price of admission. But if you can pass that test, opportunities abound if you choose to pursue them. No two Visible Experts travel the same path to prominence. Each has a unique set of strengths and weaknesses. No single personality type, family background or educational achievement guarantees success. However, we've noticed four traits that make success far more likely.

1. DEDICATION TO GROWING YOUR PROFESSIONAL EXPERTISE

Experts with intellectual curiosity and a passion for their area of specialty have an advantage over those who lack these characteristics. If you are motivated to pursue them, you can find opportunities everywhere to deepen your expertise and broaden your perspective. Carl Elefante says, "Hardly a day goes by that I don't stumble upon an article on a topic I didn't expect to be relevant but which turns out to be directly helpful to the mission I am on." Kimberly Ellison-Taylor has a similar experience: "I make it a practice to try to learn something in every environment. I want to be a sponge. And that means looking for connections that will strengthen and expand my thinking." In Chapter 7, we'll explore many ways that experts can hone their expertise.

2. WILLINGNESS TO SHARE YOUR EXPERTISE

Expertise is invisible. You can't determine someone's area of expertise just by looking at them. Without context, people have no idea what problems experts can help them solve or know when to refer them to someone else who has a need. Unless you share your expertise in some way—through writing, networking or public speaking—you will remain an invisible expert. That's why all Visible Experts are teachers at heart. While a few experts are part-time or full-time college professors, that's not the kind of teaching we mean. What we are talking about is a less formal, more organic kind of teaching. The kind that happens when you write blog posts, speak at conferences, conduct webinars or host podcasts. Whenever experts do these things, they are giving away a little bit of their expertise, usually for free.

Most experts we interviewed love teaching. They speak of "seeing the light go on" when they explain a complex new concept or deliver a game-changing insight to their audience. Remember Nishith Desai and his enthusiasm for shaping the next generation of legal talent and making the world a better place through their expertise? As Kimberly Ellison-Taylor puts it, "I love having the opportunity to work with students and next-generation leaders. I love the opportunity to help people become the best versions of themselves."

...FIRMS THAT HAVE ONE OR MORE VISIBLE EXPERTS ON THEIR TEAM ARE ABLE TO COMMAND THE HIGHEST INDUSTRY FEES.

This book will show you how to develop and execute a plan to make your expertise visible, a plan tailored to your specific strengths and limitations. We'll explain in detail how to develop your Visibility Plan in Chapters 3–5.

3. DISCIPLINE TO CREATE AND FOLLOW A PLAN

Our research shows that consistently following a plan can dramatically accelerate your Visible Expert ascent. If it usually takes experts five years to raise their visibility one level, you can reduce that time to about a year by following a Visible Expert plan. But it takes discipline to bring your plan to fruition.

Each of the experts you meet in this book had that discipline, though they didn't have the luxury of learning from the mistakes and successes of others. As Michael Zipursky, a Visible Expert you will meet in chapter 3, says, "You don't get to be a Visible Expert if you're not consistent. You don't write just one article or give one talk and then, all of a sudden, people consider you an expert. Usually, it takes a whole body of work and a great deal of time, thought and effort to achieve that level of success." Of course, most Visible Experts in our study also encountered obstacles along the way, and they had to adjust their plans as circumstances and their interests changed. In Chapter 6, we'll discuss strategies to overcome barriers that can impede your progress and what adjustments you can make to keep on track.

4. CONFIDENCE TO TAKE A POSITION

Most Visible Experts, especially those at higher visibility levels, can strengthen their reputations by taking a position on important issues. According to Kimberly Ellison-Taylor, "It means having a point of view and being unafraid of taking a stand that's controversial. When you are a Visible Expert, you have permission to be bold, to make predictions—to say not what people want to hear but what they need to hear." Reflecting on his role in shaping the way people talk about the built environment and sustainability, Carl Elefante says," There are two things that have allowed me to do this. One is my long career as an architect working with existing buildings. There is credibility that comes with that. The other is my love of a good fight, jumping in when there is an opportunity to get engaged and make a difference." Of course, everyone's journey to prominence is different. In the next chapter, we'll explore the process of choosing your niche and deciding which style of sharing your expertise is right for you.

> VISIBLE EXPERTS ARE TEACHERS AT HEART.

» A revolution is reshaping the professional services. It is driven by soaring demand, the increased visibility of specialized expertise and the erosion of geography as a constraint on providing services.

» These factors dramatically increase the role that high-profile experts play in the marketing and delivery of professional services. We call these individuals Visible Experts.

» There are five distinct levels of visibility, each with higher degrees of influence and earning potential.

» Visible Experts benefit from strong personal brands, greater opportunities and exceptional career flexibility.

» Visible Experts also benefit the professional services firms that employ them through a psychological principle called the halo effect.

CHAPTER TWO

CLAIM YOUR NICHE.

DEVELOP YOUR PERSPECTIVE.

THE FIRST STEP IN YOUR JOURNEY TO BECOMING A TRUE VISIBLE EXPERT IS TO FIND AND CLEARLY DEFINE YOUR NICHE. What exactly are you an expert in? Who is your target audience? And how will that audience benefit from your expertise?

Here's how Rachel Fisch, a Toronto-based Visible Expert with an international reputation, describes her work: "I live at the intersection of accounting and technology. I work with technology companies to help them better understand accountants and how to market to them. And I also work with accounting firms to help them implement technology." But she doesn't stop there. She is particularly interested in the application of technology to specific areas of accounting. Rachel is an example of what we call a Laser: someone who has a sharply defined field of expertise. Highly focused expertise is a powerful strategy used by many high-visibility subject matter experts.

The Laser is one of five Visible Expert styles that we will cover in this chapter. Understanding which style suits your personality can help you determine the focus of your expertise. For some people the answer will be obvious. They already have an established field of expertise and a well-researched target audience. But for many subject matter experts, the answers are not always clear. In this chapter, we'll explore some of the key considerations that go into selecting your focus.

HOW RACHEL FOUND HER NICHE

Rachel, who was trained as an accounting professional, was running her own small firm when she began to realize that her passion for technology could be applied to her job. "I started getting interested in technology, especially the way accountants could leverage it. That was several years ago now, when the cloud was still new." Many professionals have similar experiences. Something seemingly unrelated to their day job captures their imagination. For many would-be experts, that's as far as it goes. But Rachel realized that her general interest in technology could be applied to her profession. She was then able to bring those two interests together into a specialized niche. But she didn't stop there.

"I've taken it a step further and really focused narrowly on a specific niche within accounting and technology," says Rachel. She concentrated her expertise on the use of technology in bookkeeping and client advisory services. "That means I can get even more focused on the technology that we use. I can get more specific on the accounting needs of that market." That additional step has given her an advantage that accelerated her career. "What I've learned is that once you focus deeply in an area, you really become in demand as a speaker and educator. You are marrying your visibility and expertise in a specific niche with a specific need. So, when conferences or event planners are looking for somebody to speak on a specific topic, they know that Rachel Fisch is their person for that topic."

> IF YOU TRY TO BE AN EXPERT IN EVERYTHING YOU WILL END UP BEING AN EXPERT IN NOTHING.

THE POWER OF FOCUS

Rachel has learned to leverage the power of focus. By narrowing your focus you can accelerate your success. The benefits of having a narrow focus are nicely captured in a TED talk by international author, speaker and digital marketing innovator Seth Godin. "The idea you create, the product you create—it's not for everyone," says Seth. "It's not a mass thing. That's not what this is about. What it's about instead is finding the true believers." These "true believers" will then become your advocates and grow your brand for you. Focus also gives you an angle to challenge conventional thinking and established methods. True thought leaders often hold strong opinions and take unexpected positions. Having narrowly defined expertise gives you a platform to promote your ideas.

Our research on Visible Experts shows that those with the fastest rise to prominence were three times as likely to have a narrowly defined niche. They were also more likely to adopt this focus earlier in their career.

TWO STRATEGIES TO INCREASE YOUR FOCUS

There are two basic strategies to increase your focus. The first is to narrow the scope of your expertise. This is the strategy that Rachel Fisch used so successfully. Rather than trying to take on the many ways accounting and technology intersect, she tightly narrowed her focus on a specific niche: bookkeeping and client advisory services. This allowed her to master the subject matter more quickly and thoroughly—and made it easier for her audience to understand what she does and exactly where Rachel's expertise is relevant.

The second strategy is to be among the first to enter an area of focus. Think of this as a first mover advantage. The sooner you focus on a field, the easier it is to become visible in that realm of expertise. You may recall how Nishith Desai, whom we met in Chapter 1, built an international law firm by establishing expertise in emerging areas of the law. Because his firm was the first to embrace that strategy, it was able to establish its credentials and grow its visibility before their competitors caught on.

Visible Expert Mark Amtower recognizes the value of being an early entrant into his niche, marketing consulting for businesses that sell to the government. "I was fortunate that when I started writing about marketing to the federal government nobody else was," recalls Mark. "Nobody was treating it as a separate discipline, so when I started The Amtower Report in 1991, I had an instant audience. My problem was distribution because we used snail mail. I ended up mailing about 7,000 newsletters each month, and that got a little pricey. But it established me as a person who was thinking about, writing about and watching what was happening in marketing to the government. That led to me being invited to speak at events and writing more. It got me a column in Washington

Technology, which I've been writing for fourteen years. It's the reason Federal News Radio (now Federal News Network) reached out to have me do their first show for the government contracting community. Prior to my presence there, the station was exclusively for federal employees. I've been on the radio for sixteen years. I've got nine books out. I write for a variety of publications. My stuff gets picked up."

Mark's thinking has never stopped evolving. As the marketplace and technology change, so does his approach. For example, he was an early adopter of LinkedIn, and he has developed deep expertise in using the platform to reach the government marketplace. "I was a beta user of Pulse," says Mark. "I've been writing on LinkedIn for about eight years now. I have well over 200 articles on the LinkedIn platform. So the visibility factor is there. I've been a focal point for marketing to the government for almost four decades."

Mark's early entry into the marketplace, his visibility and his ability to evolve with changing times have made Mark the pre-eminent thought leader in marketing to the government and drive his ongoing success.

FIND YOUR AREA OF FOCUS

One of your key decisions will be to choose your area of focus. In other words, what are you an expert in? And how do you want people to remember you so they can refer you to someone who might need your services?

As we've learned from Rachel Fisch, Nishith Desai and Mark Amtower, choosing the right area of focus can have a positive— even dramatic—impact on your career. Get it wrong, however, and you'll struggle to find the visibility and create the reputation that you desire. But if you narrow your focus too much, there won't be enough demand for you to thrive. Clearly, finding the right balance is critical.

To help you find your area of focus, we've developed a series of five criteria. We suggest that you consider each of these as you determine a possible area of specialization. As we present these criteria, we will include some examples from the professional services realm. However, the same criteria still apply if we were to target cultural or societal issues, as Carl Elefante, whom we introduced in Chapter 1, does with his focus on sustainability and the built environment.

CRITERION 1: IS YOUR FOCUS NARROW ENOUGH TO BE EFFECTIVE?

If you try to be an expert in everything you will end up being an expert in nothing. Your area of focus should not be so broad that you can't master the subject matter or build credibility with your target audience. For example, suppose you work in a public accounting firm. Specializing in taxes would probably be too ambitious, even counterproductive. Why? Because there are many levels of taxation, from local and state to national and international. There are also many different types of taxes, including value-added tax, sales tax and income tax. To specialize in all of those disciplines is not only a huge task, your audience may find it hard to believe that a single person could be an expert in every area of tax.

> ONE OF YOUR KEY DECISIONS WILL BE TO CHOOSE YOUR AREA OF FOCUS.

How do you narrow your focus? One way would be to specialize in a particular level of taxation—such as international taxes. This might be a smart move if you work with companies that conduct business across international borders. As you may recall, this was the specialization that Nishith Desai used when he achieved his initial success as a Visible Expert. Or you could specialize in a particular type of taxes, such as estate taxes. This is a narrow enough niche that you could credibly claim to be an expert in it—and have a reasonable chance of keeping abreast of any new regulations and future legislation.

CRITERION 2: IS IT BROAD ENOUGH THAT THERE IS ENOUGH DEMAND?

If spreading your focus too wide can be problematic, so can going too far in the other direction. If you choose an area that is too narrow, you may struggle to find enough clients to support your practice. Often, this issue can be solved by expanding your target geographic market. For example, a relatively small niche, such as cybersecurity for public utilities, may not be viable if you work only in your immediate local area. There may not be enough potential clients—and revenue—to achieve your business goals. However, if you were to expand your marketplace to include your region or even the entire country, you might have more than enough clients. In Criterion 4 below, we describe one way you may be able to determine whether or not your area of focus is too narrow.

CRITERION 3: IS IT RELEVANT TO YOUR AUDIENCE?

While it's important to choose an area of specialization that interests you and supports your overall goals, it is just as important to select one that is relevant to your audience. What if the public utilities you targeted in the example above are reluctant to invest in cybersecurity? To know that requires a deep understanding of your target audience. In Chapter 3, we will discuss how you can develop this level of understanding.

Until you do the due diligence, you may not know whether your target audience even cares about your new area of focus. If you ultimately determine there is little interest in your area and you cannot change your audience, you may need to consider adjusting your specialization to enhance its relevance. If, however, you have the flexibility to change your target, you may be able to look for a different niche audience with whom your specialization resonates. If your area of focus doesn't check the box for this criterion you could waste a lot of energy and fail to produce the results you're looking for.

CRITERION 4: DO OTHER EXPERTS SERVE THIS AUDIENCE?

This is an interesting and counterintuitive criterion. At first, you might think of other experts in your field as competitors—and people to keep at arm's length. In a niche oversaturated with experts that might be true. But in our research, we found that the situation is almost always more complicated and nuanced. The very existence of experts who share your area of focus can be a signal that you have stumbled upon a viable niche. This is especially helpful if you have concerns that the niche you are considering is too small to sustain a practice. In addition, you may be able to find other Visible Experts who can help you grow as a professional. We cover this topic in detail in Chapter 7. Developing good working relationships with other Visible Experts in your area of expertise can also be an important way to generate new business opportunities. Many established Visible Experts, for instance, receive far more speaking invitations than they can handle, and they are often more than happy to refer the overflow to someone they know and respect. Many are also approached with opportunities that fall outside of their narrow area of focus, a common situation which can provide more referrals.

CRITERION 5: DO YOU HAVE A NOVEL APPROACH?

Specializing in a particular area is an important first step. However, if you're going to realize your full potential as a Visible Expert you likely will need a unique perspective or a novel approach. Regular experts generate minimal visibility because they have nothing new or interesting to say. Visible Experts, however, have a point of view that is all their own.

How do you find your unique voice? Where does your novel perspective come from? This is one of our most fascinating findings. In many cases, that perspective comes from within—who you are as a person and how you interact with your audience and your subject matter. We call these behavior patterns your Visible Expert style. To explain what we mean, let's see how three experts created very different approaches to similar subject matter.

A TALE OF THREE EXPERTS

The junction of accounting and technology is a broad and active field. We have profiled three Visible Experts who approach this topic in very different ways. The approach taken by each expert very much reflects their individual styles and personalities.

We turn first to Kimberly Ellison-Taylor, whom you met in Chapter 1. Kimberly is what we call a Bridge Builder. She treats accounting as a particular application of technology. As a Bridge Builder she also looks at how technology can be applied to other industries. This helps her connect different disciplines and find commonalities and synergies that not everyone sees.

Rachel Fisch takes an altogether different approach. Rather than focusing on connections between multiple subject matter domains, Rachel has chosen to go deeper and specialize in a particular type of accounting and the technologies that can make it better. We call this narrowly focused style a Laser. Where Kimberly adopted a relatively broad focus, Rachel drills deep with a very narrow specialization.

Then there's Jody Padar. Jody has branded herself as The Radical CPA. Always on the lookout for the newest thing, she positions herself as a pioneer exploring the leading-edge technologies that will transform the profession of accounting. We call this style a First Mover—and her approach is quite distinct from Rachel's and Kimberly's.

What does this mean for you? If you can identify your personal style and what comes naturally to you, your approach to your subject matter—and what kind of a Visible Expert you want to be—will become clearer. So next, let's explore the five signature Visible Expert styles.

THE FIVE VISIBLE EXPERT STYLES

During our research we identified five distinct Visible Expert styles. In some cases, experts were clearly influenced by styles outside of their primary one. We call these secondary styles. Figure 2.1 describes each style and the proportion of Visible Experts in our study who identified each as their primary style. The most common style is The Bridge Builder, representing over forty-five percent of experts. The Contrarian was the least prevalent, representing less than one in ten experts. Let's look at examples of each style and how they shaped real-world experts' careers.

» The Five Visible Expert Styles

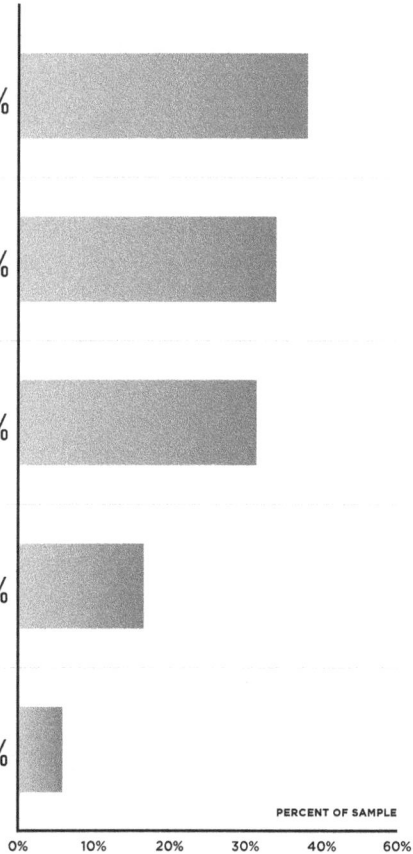

The Bridge Builder
This expert spans two different areas of expertise, connecting ideas from both. This combination of knowledge makes this expert truly unique.
46.0%

The Laser
This expert is highly specialized in a very specific area. Not many businesses need their services all the time, but when the time comes, this is the preferred choice.
41.0%

The Curator
This expert gathers the best information from multiple sources. Often, Curators have access to an extensive network of experts.
38.0%

The First Mover
This expert was the first to pioneer an area of expertise. Businesses turn to First Movers for the latest innovation or new idea.
20.0%

The Contrarian
This expert takes novel points of view on industry issues and challenges clients to make bold or unconventional moves.
14.0%

PERCENT OF SAMPLE

0%   10%   20%   30%   40%   60%

FIGURE 2.1

THE BRIDGE BUILDER

Kimberly Ellison-Taylor is a perfect example of The Bridge Builder. As she explains, "I am definitely a Bridge Builder style expert. And by Bridge Builder, I mean I connect the dots between many fields of expertise. I see things, sometimes, that other people may not see because I can look at other industries, whether it's financial services, oil and gas, manufacturing or healthcare and identify the things they're doing extremely well. I can then bring those ideas to other industries and other professions that may be facing similar challenges.

"I think the ability to do that takes some political acumen. It means having an industry point of view. It means being unafraid of saying something that people may be uncomfortable about. And that gives you a platform of responsibility. And that platform of responsibility means that you have to stay current. It means that if you're building bridges between multiple levels of competencies that you have to stay current. There's no way to say that I stand at the intersection of technology and accounting and people and not continue to reinforce that level of understanding for each one of those areas."

THE LASER

Rachel Fisch, too, sees herself as a Bridge Builder between the realms of accounting and technology. But as we learned earlier, much of her success has come from her laser-like focus on the bookkeeping function. Rachel explains, "I got into the accounting technology world out of curiosity and a fascination with the technology that was being employed within the accounting industry. Being able to leverage that as a user, extend it to my clients and then train other bookkeepers and accountants to use those same tools seemed like a natural extension of the service that I wanted to provide."

This laser focus on a specific niche has bestowed her with the benefits of hyper-specialization: "Since then, I've worked almost exclusively with technology. I've learned to fine-tune workflows and tech stacks so that everything is optimized and is a really good experience for us and our clients."

THE CURATOR

Mark Amtower captures the essence of how The Curator style works: "Writing about what other people are doing, absorbing what I learned and then applying those lessons to my customers' situations is what I've been doing since day one." Mark's radio program and regular columns give him multiple channels to share the insights of his guests, who are experts in their own right. It has also given him access to a very broad range of ideas. "Maybe two or three things have come up that are 'original' in over thirty-seven years. I think that's pretty good because there's not much that's original out there. It's adapting what works for other people and understanding where it could fit."

In many ways, Mark is performing a very valuable service to his followers. He combs through a broad swath of information to capture the most valuable insights. He not only saves his readers and listeners valuable time, he adds his perspective to the challenges they face. Mark also brings this wealth of knowledge and experience to his clients. "I've got thirty-seven years of this otherwise useless data in my head. If you ask me a marketing problem—and my mentees do—I go back into that treasure trove, and we come up with an answer that works for them and their situation."

THE FIRST MOVER

We have already met two examples of First Movers. Nishith Desai built an entire firm of Visible Experts—a firm that was the first to focus on emerging areas of the law, especially as it applies to technology and social change. Jody Padar is another great example of a First Mover. She embraces the latest thinking and newest ideas. She describes herself as a pioneer. And she relishes her moniker, The Radical CPA. It suits her well.

"I'm the one who runs ahead then looks back," says Jody. "Usually there's no one behind me, which is hard sometimes. You want to be that innovator, yet the rest of the market is still ten steps behind you." It can be hard for a First Mover to slow down and get in sync with audiences that are trailing behind. "It's kind of funny. What they're talking about today is the kind of the firm that I invented fifteen years ago," she says. "That's what people today *think* is the new firm. But that was new ten years ago, right? And now I'm on to what's next. There's a small subset of people who want to be here—at what's next. Most people are still back with that vision from a decade ago. About ten percent of my audience wants what's next and ninety percent of my audience wants tried-and-true stuff that I've been talking about for the last ten years. So, when you're talking to your audience, it's hard because you know that you must serve both parts of it." As we've found with many experts, Jody also has a secondary style: "I'm also a Bridge Builder between accountancy and technology or tax and technology. But mostly, I'm a pioneer."

THE CONTRARIAN

Rhondalynn Korolak has a fascinating background. Trained in finance and accounting, she had a high-profile career in tax law with Canada's largest law firm and a Big-Four accounting firm. Changes in her personal life led her to immigrate to Australia. That's when her career began to evolve. She became interested in business growth and cash flow. She found that entrepreneurs and small business owners were most impacted by these issues, and her interventions had a transformative effect on these organizations, which she found exhilarating. This discovery led to the ultimate focus of her career— helping small and emerging businesses master their cash flow challenges and achieve extraordinary growth.

"I suspect I have a little bit of First Mover, Contrarian, and Bridge Builder in me," says Rhondalynn. "But The Contrarian is definitely the strongest. The entire financial industry was talking about cash flow in terms of fintech products and dashboards. I've never thought that way. Right from the start, ten years ago, I was well ahead of my time. I knew that traditional view wasn't going to cut the mustard. And I know that I'm right about that because we haven't seen cash flow tackled and solved yet as a problem."

"For me," she continues, "this whole contrarian thing is really important because what we have been doing doesn't work. Teaching people numbers, dashboarding the daylights out of people, having all these fintech products that have twenty-four-percent interest rates and look exactly like credit cards but are being called small business loans—that's not working. A viable solution is to help people change their mindset around money. If you've got 'stinking thinking'—that's my technical term—or a chronic poverty mindset, a scarcity mentality or a belief that you're not good enough, these unproductive thoughts will drive your results. If you don't change your mindset first, then implement systems to fix your cash flow problems, you will inadvertently sabotage yourself."

To remedy these problems, she focuses on two things: First, she addresses people's mindsets so that they are prepared mentally to be bountiful and successful. Second, she teaches complex financial concepts in a fun, easy-to-understand way that makes her clients feel confident, competent and good about themselves. "So that's the contrarian in me."

CREATE YOUR EXPERT PROFILE

In this chapter, we've laid down five criteria to determine if you have a powerful focus. We've also identified the five Visible Expert styles. Now it is time for you to apply these concepts to your situation.

You will capture this information in a concise paragraph called your expert profile. If you were a firm, you might call this your positioning statement. Your expert profile will become the foundation of your new brand—and a primary source for your messaging. It is a place to describe your specialized expertise, how you apply it to help your clients and your overall positioning. It needs to communicate just three things:

1. **What you do**
2. **Who you do it for**
3. **The biggest benefit of working with you**

To capture these details crisply, your expert profile should be short—as few as two or three sentences long. Begin by thinking about your area of focus and what key benefits clients experience when they work with you. Then review the five Visible Expert styles and determine which of them best describes your approach. For example, if you are primarily a First Mover, you may want to emphasize how your clients rely on you to understand the latest developments in your field.

Carl Elefante's primary style is Bridge Builder and his secondary style is First Mover. Here's how he might write his profile:

> **I was one of the first architects to merge the disciplines of historic preservation and sustainability. I am changing the way today's architects think about existing buildings and how to use them in a way that is environmentally sound, inspiring and equitable.**

Mark Amtower is a Curator at heart, with a First Mover secondary style. His expert profile might look something like this:

> **As one of the first to specialize in marketing to the government, I am a leading consultant to government contractors who want to connect with federal buyers. For thirty-seven years I have interviewed government buyers and sellers to learn what tools and techniques are most effective. Everything I write and teach my clients is informed by this deep body of experience.**

Start with a preliminary draft of your expert profile. Don't worry about getting it perfect right now. In Chapter 3, you'll learn how to use your research to help to refine the way you position yourself.

» Identify your area of professional focus, target audiences and expertise style. These are important foundational elements of a successful Visible Expert strategy.

» The narrower your niche or the earlier you become active in an emerging field, the easier it will be to elevate the visibility of your expertise.

» There are five distinct Visible Expert styles. Build on your natural strengths and select a style that fits your interests, personality and approach.

» Use these insights to draft your Expert Profile. This process will uncover your positioning and help you talk about yourself with greater clarity and consistency.

» This preliminary draft should describe what you do, who you do it for and how your clients benefit from working with you. You can use the research we explain in Chapter 3 to refine it.

CHAPTER THREE

RESEARCH
YOUR
AUDIENCE

VISIBLE EXPERTS ARE AT THEIR STRONGEST WHEN THEY HAVE A CLEAR AND OBJECTIVE UNDERSTANDING OF THEIR MARKETPLACE. But this insight doesn't simply come with experience. In fact, experience can distort one's perspective, and it can be difficult to separate reality from perceptions shaped by anecdotes, hearsay and long-held assumptions.

The surest way to get a clearer vision of your market is to conduct research into your target audience. While some experts can do this research on their own—think back to Nishith Desai and his personal quest to understand the legal and professional landscape around him—you will probably need help. For most Visible Experts, this support comes from their firms, which have the financial and professional resources to carry out a high-quality study. But even firms usually need additional support from a third party research consultant that knows how to conduct a meaningful, valid study. And because they have no skin in the game and are more likely to be seen as impartial, these outsiders are able to extract more honest responses from your audience than if you or someone on your staff were asking the questions.

What if you are a solo practitioner with limited funds? Is research out of reach? Not at all. But you may have to do much of the work yourself. And you may have to take some shortcuts. Even a simple online survey of your clients—if it's crafted with care—can provide a wealth of information and insights.

"WOULD YOU PLEASE GET ME FIRED?"

Dan Adams didn't start out wanting to become a Visible Expert. "I think some people may set out to become a Visible Expert but that wasn't me at all. I had spent twenty-nine years working inside of large corporations. I thought they were going to bury me in the backyard when they were done with me." But one day, Dan had an epiphany—one that led to a most unusual request. "I was working in the innovation space and there were some things we were doing that were actually working. It was very exciting, and I thought,

'You know what? I just want to go for it.' I went to my boss and said, 'Would you please get me fired?' I did that because I wanted to get a severance package to get me started. I didn't really know what I was getting into at all."

Dan left to build the AIM Institute, a firm with a very specialized expertise. "Clients hire us to help them with their new product development. They're usually Fortune 500 companies with a B2B market focus."

RESEARCH GIVES YOU VALUABLE INSIGHT INTO YOUR TARGET AUDIENCE AND ELIMINATES MUCH OF THE GUESSWORK AS YOU DEVELOP YOUR PLAN.

To understand Dan's value as a Visible Expert, you need to know a bit about his business. "If you think about developing the next hydraulic cylinder or the next polymer, there are two things you must do well," says Dan. "First, you must figure out what it is the customers really want. Second, you must have some bright engineers, chemists and scientists to make it. Turns out that most of our clients are really good at the second thing and they're really bad at the first thing. They just don't know what their customers want, at least not to the level they could. So, we're basically in the training business. We go to our clients and we teach their chemists, scientists, marketers and salespeople how to interview these professional B2B people and really understand what their needs are."

But communicating this complex message in a concise and compelling way proved to be a challenge. "We knew what we were doing for them, but we weren't really clear how to explain it succinctly. If I've got half an hour to explain it to you, I probably can get that across. If I've got a very short time, like on a website, I need to be crystal clear."

TWO REASONS TO DO RESEARCH

Dan's dilemma is one that many aspiring experts face. Long years of relevant experience had given him the core expertise and market familiarity to advise his clients with confidence. But that kind of knowledge can also be a barrier. It's easy to convince yourself that you know everything already when, in reality, you are too close to your subject matter to be objective. Research can provide the objectivity that you need. In fact, there are two great reasons to conduct your own research.

REASON 1: RESEARCH GIVES YOU INSIGHT

Dan explains how research helped his firm overcome this barrier. "The journey began with some research. Our research firm, Hinge, went out and talked to our clients. They didn't have that curse of thinking that we already had the answers. And they were able to find out what our clients were really seeking—and why they were coming to us. We asked them to interview some clients who love us, some clients who stopped using us and some clients in between. When that work was done, we had a much better picture of how we should explain what it is we do. That was the starting point for us."

Dan's story nicely illustrates the first key benefit of research: Research gives you valuable insight into your target audience and eliminates much of the guesswork as you develop your plan. This insight will inform the way you talk about your expertise, the services you offer and the marketing channels you use. But that's not all. There is an equally compelling second benefit.

REASON 2: RESEARCH IS VALUABLE CONTENT

Like you, many of your potential clients and referral sources are eager to learn about their competitors and how *they* handle common industry challenges. As a result, the research you do for yourself can have a second life—as valuable content. Research can fuel a powerful thought-leadership marketing campaign. You can use it as the foundation for blog posts, social media posts, webinars, speeches and more. And you may even want to conduct additional research for just this purpose. In a world where objectivity is often difficult to find, data can be a powerful differentiator.

Dan Adams explains how his firm has benefited by using its research as content. "One thing that's been a pleasant surprise for us is that you can do a modest amount of research and just keep using it over and over again."

He cites a specific example. "We reached out to our clients and others in the marketplace. They took a survey on the growth drivers in their business—things like interviewing their customers, having a Stage-Gate® process or group patenting of their novel concepts in the lab. We came up with twenty-four growth drivers and asked clients how important each was for their growth and how satisfied they were. This quantitative information has been tremendously useful because now we can publish all kinds of charts and graphs and so forth. We're able to compare the companies that didn't do well with the companies that did do well. What were the biggest differentiators? It became content for newsletters, whitepapers and research reports. We used it in videos. It's a wonderful topic for our conferences. People love it."

Dan Adams is not the only Visible Expert who appreciates the power of research. Take Michael Zipursky, for example. Michael is the CEO and co-founder of Consulting Success, a firm that works with entrepreneurial consultants to help them build more profitable, scalable and strategic consulting businesses.

According to Michael, high-value content like research has powered his business' success. "About thirteen years ago, when we started Consulting Success, we were still running our consulting business on the side while sharing ideas with other consultants. That was the whole idea behind Consulting Success—to share our experiences from the trenches and help consultants avoid land mines and common mistakes so they can accelerate their business success."

As other Visible Experts have learned, sharing one's expertise attracts opportunities. "New opportunities pop up all the time.

We have organizations, professional groups and associations asking for me to speak or to contribute content or an article. People from around the world that we've never met in person reach out and say, 'I'd like to learn about one of your programs or join one of your communities or become a client,' without us having to sell to them."

This is a key insight that motivates people to create content. This kind of exposure can save you a huge amount of business development time and reduce risk. "The content that we put out is doing the heavy lifting for us," says Michael.

Where does this steady stream of insightful new content come from? In Michael's case, much of it comes from surveys, as well as conversations with clients and other people in the industry. "We conduct several surveys each year. One survey explores the area of marketing and business development in consulting. Another looks at fees and pricing strategies for consultants. We also do a survey around the lifestyle, health and wellness issues that consultants face."

RESEARCH CAN FUEL A POWERFUL THOUGHT-LEADERSHIP MARKETING CAMPAIGN.

Michael's team uses their findings in multiple ways. "We do these surveys because they help us better understand the market that we want to serve. We get a lot of ideas about what kind of content, articles, podcasts, training and new programs we might offer. We see what the market wants to learn more about and where our buyers have the greatest needs and desires."

As with Dan Adams, research gives Michael insights that are interesting to his clients and prospects. "In almost every survey, something surprises us or makes us think, okay, we need to go and explore that—open that door and dig in a little bit more to see what we can uncover and share."

Original research can play an important marketing role, too. Michael compiles the data from his surveys into reports that he shares on his website, podcast and social media. This type of research-based content is a powerful way to generate online leads and build engagement with your audience.

Clearly, conducting research on your target audience offers big benefits. But how do you actually do it? The first step in conducting any research is to determine the purpose of that research: What questions are you trying to answer? Are you trying to understand your target audience better? Do you want more referrals? Are you trying to influence public policy, your target audience, lawmakers or the general public?

The questions you want to answer will determine three things:

1. **Who your target audience should be**
2. **The type of research you will be doing**
3. **The specific questions you will ask in your research**

Let's start by looking at potential target audiences.

SELECT YOUR TARGET AUDIENCES

A target audience is any group or market segment that you are trying to reach with a specific message. Think about it this way: Which audiences already know you, and which ones do you wish knew you better? Who are you trying to influence? To help you answer these questions, let's review some of Visible Experts' most common target audiences. As you define your target audiences, think about which industries they are in, what job positions they hold and what types of organizations they work in. Keep in mind that many experts have more than one target audience.

Clients and prospects. When targeting potential clients, think especially about your best clients—the ones that appreciate your expertise and with whom it's easy to build an ongoing relationship. They need to understand how you can help them and which problems you can help them solve.

Referral sources. For most experts, referral sources are important drivers of new business. Usually, referrers are either former clients or other professionals in adjacent industries who serve a similar target audience. Think lawyers and accountants, or architects and engineers. They serve the same clientele but don't directly compete with each other. To get the most from your referral sources, you'll want to understand what motivates them to make a referral.*

Amplifiers. These are influencers who will amplify your message to your target audience. They may include industry journalists, bloggers, podcasters or even other Visible Experts. In fact, these Visible Experts may refer business to you or partner with you to provide specialized solutions. While you might think of these individuals as direct competitors, don't underestimate their potential value to you. Amplifiers not only enhance your visibility but also add credibility to your messages.

Analysts and investors. This is an important audience for public companies that are sensitive to their stock price or closely held firms that are seeking outside financing. Industry analysts cover companies within particular industries, so it can be important to be visible to this influential group. If you are a public company, regulations require that you disclose certain information. But analysts and investors also look at a variety of other information sources, as well—including what a firm's experts say in their thought leadership. So making your experts more visible may be a great opportunity to demonstrate your firm's sophistication.

---

* As you become better known, you are likely to receive referrals from people you've never even met—on the strength of your reputation or thought leadership alone.

Public opinion. Not all Visible Experts are solely focused on developing business for their professional practice. Some have larger personal goals that involve important issues such as social justice or environmental stewardship. Kimberly Ellison-Taylor and Carl Elefante, whom you met in the first chapter, are examples of experts who are using their visibility and expertise to influence public policy.

Take a few minutes to review the list above and select the target audiences that you believe are most important to your success as a Visible Expert. If you have multiple target audiences, as most experts do, try to order them by level of priority. At this point, your list is still preliminary. As you move through the research process you may uncover new information that causes you to rethink your earlier choices.

THREE TYPES OF RESEARCH

For our purposes, there are three types of research you might use to understand your audience and marketplace. The first is original research, which is often called **primary research**. In this type of research you collect original data from your target audience, typically in the form of surveys or structured interviews.

The second type of research, called **secondary research**, uses data that has already been gathered by others. For instance, you might examine relevant existing studies from professional research firms, trade associations, government entities or other organizations that collect data on your audience.

The third type of research is **informal research**. Usually, this involves gathering and systematically reviewing information that comes from your own organization. For example, you might talk to everyone in your firm who is involved in business development to find out what issues your clients are most concerned about. If you are a solo expert, it could be as simple as keeping notes over time about your clients' evolving business problems. You might also look at your sales history to determine what services or products your clients are buying, and in what quantities. If you think carefully about your business, you will likely find a number of places you can collect internal data and analyze it for insights. While informal research lacks the scientific rigor of a formal study, it can be very helpful when other data simply is not available. Just be aware of its limitations as you use it.

WHICH TYPE OF RESEARCH SHOULD YOU USE?

Which of these three types of research is right for you? In fact, there's a very good chance you will need different types of research to answer different questions. To understand why, let's look at the example of Nishith Desai Associates (NDA), the global law firm with many Visible Experts.

Their experts use secondary research from well regarded consulting firms to help them identify interesting trends. But they also perform informal research with clients and outside subject matter experts to help them decide which trends are worth further study. At that point they dive into an issue's legal implications, using both secondary and informal research to build a deeper understanding and formulate an approach to the issue. NDA also uses primary research. For example, they retained our firm to help them understand the strength of their brand and measure their client experience.

Let's explore each type of research in more detail so you can determine which type is right for your situation.

Primary research. Primary research is what most people think of when they hear the term research. It involves conducting an original study on an audience of your choosing by asking a series of questions designed to answer your most pressing questions. Because it can be tailored and narrowly targeted, primary research is usually the most relevant and actionable type of research.

Most Visible Experts conduct this kind of research using either an online survey or structured interviews. A structured interview is an oral interview in which the questions are determined ahead of time and asked in a specific order, allowing you to gather the same information across all people interviewed.

You can approach primary research in two ways: you can conduct it yourself, or you can hire an independent researcher or organization to do it for you. The benefit of doing it yourself is that you have more control over the process—and it is less expensive. The surveys conducted by Michael Zipursky, whom we met earlier in this chapter, are examples of self-administered primary research. Doing the research yourself works well when your research subjects may be less concerned about remaining anonymous. If, however, they have privacy or confidentiality concerns, using an independent research organization is probably a better choice. That said, it is possible to conduct surveys without collecting personal information—in fact, Michael's team keeps their results strictly anonymous. Just be aware that self-administered research may be perceived by participants as less impartial than that conducted by an outside resource.

You will also need to ask yourself whether you or your organization has the expertise and time to conduct and analyze research data. Designing a valid survey, interviewing subjects and turning raw data into something useful require skill. If you do not have those capabilities in-house, consider using a third-party research organization, instead.

If you are surveying current or past clients, an independent research organization will almost always produce more honest and valuable insights. The promise of anonymity allows people to speak freely without fear that their identities and specific responses will be revealed to your organization. This was the circumstance that Dan Adams faced—and why he used a third party to conduct the research. He was concerned that clients might be less candid if they talked directly to someone within his firm.

Secondary research. Secondary research has two big advantages: you usually can get access to it quickly, and it costs much less than an original study. But it has a significant downside, too:

you only have access to data that already exists. You can't add a topic, customize the audience or modify a question. You have to work with what is available.

Secondary research is particularly useful when you're looking for population-level data. For example, if you want to know how many of a certain type of manufacturing business operates within a specific geographical region, government census data might provide just the answer you need. Or if you want to understand how a particular industry is performing, look for analysts' reports or trade association data that can give you a lay of the land. Figure 3.1 lists several places that you might look for relevant secondary research.

Secondary Research Sources

ONLINE SEARCHES	SOCIAL MEDIA LISTENING
BOOKS	ANALYST REPORTS
JOURNALS	GOVERNMENT REPORTS
TRADE ASSOCIATIONS & NONPROFITS	

FIGURE 3.1

Informal research. We call this informal research because it is either anecdotal or involves data collected for another purpose. For example, you might look at your own firm's financial records and determine that your most profitable clients often come from the same two industries. What do they have in common? You might gather anecdotal information by systematically polling your sales team or asking for input from client-facing professionals within your organization. While not up to the rigorous statistical standards of a formal study, this type of research is still better than relying on one person's general impression of the marketplace. Why? By compiling anecdotal information from a range of people, you minimize the distortions that can be introduced by a single source of information.

However imperfect, this process will give you a better feel for how your clients really behave. Informal research also has the advantage of being relatively quick and inexpensive to gather. This makes it well suited to smaller firms and individual experts—and a great starting place before considering secondary or primary research.

WHAT QUESTIONS ARE YOU TRYING TO ANSWER?

The type of research you conduct will be driven by the questions you want to answer. Usually, it will be obvious which approach is most likely to provide the answer you need. For instance, if you want to understand broad industry trends, secondary research is likely to be the fastest and most affordable way to access that information. But if you want to understand how your target audience thinks— or how that thinking has changed recently—primary research is the way to go, though informal research might get you in the ballpark.

So what are some of the most important questions you'll want to answer on your journey to Visible Expertise? Here are some of our favorites.

What are the biggest challenges that your clients face? When you have a grasp of the really big business issues that your clients and prospects wrestle with, you have a powerful tool that you can put to work in two ways. First, you can use this knowledge to capture their attention by focusing your content marketing on topics that are highly relevant to them. Second, you can look for areas where your expertise can address one or more of their business issues. Put another way, what are the most important issues that you can help your clients solve?

Where else would they go to find solutions to their challenges? This question begins to address the competitive environment. If your client didn't come to you to address their issue, where would they go? They might, for instance, seek out a specific competitor, try to solve the problem internally or choose to leave the problem unsolved entirely. This information can help you identify who and what you are competing against.

How do you compare to your competitors? Answers to this question can help you understand your competitive advantage.

Who does your target audience consider your competitors? What do you do differently than other experts or service providers? Does your Visible Expertise differentiate you from your top competitors? What existing differences could you strengthen?

Where do your potential clients look for business-related information and advice? This question can help you select the best channels to reach your target audience. What social media platforms do they use for business purposes? What blogs do they follow? What conferences do they attend? Where do they look for webinars and other educational events? Are they more inclined to read something or to watch a video? When you understand where and how your clients look for business-related insights and information you can position yourself to be more visible in those channels.

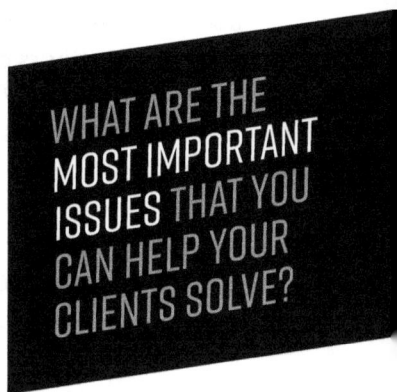

> WHAT ARE THE MOST IMPORTANT ISSUES THAT YOU CAN HELP YOUR CLIENTS SOLVE?

Why do your best clients choose you? Clients consider a host of things when selecting a professional to work with. The purpose of this question is to find out what it takes to tip the scale in your favor. Put another way, why do your very best clients select you rather than one of your competitors? Once you have some answers, you will be able to create a credentials package (see Chapter 5) that is more relevant and highlights the factors that are most important to decision makers.

What is the real value you provide to your clients? We all like to believe that we deliver great value to our clients. This question helps you understand whether your clients agree and what they value most about you and your service. In many cases, you'll find that clients value different things than you expect. Research can uncover things that you do differently than other experts and which aspects of your service delivery are most meaningful to your audience.

UNDERSTANDING YOUR COMPETITIVE ENVIRONMENT

One of the more interesting aspects of the Visible Expert space is the role that competitors play. Forget how you normally think about competitors. It's more nuanced than that. As we learned earlier, competitors can sometimes also be allies, and that is particularly true of Visible Experts. There are just two different kinds of competitors that matter to these individuals. Let's look at each briefly.

Direct competitors. Direct competitors are other businesses that offer similar services. They may have their own Visible Experts. You will want to understand who these competitors are to be able to learn from their experience and identify how you are different from them. Understanding these traits will allow you to differentiate yourself in a meaningful way.

Indirect competitors. In the expert space there are also other organizations that offer thought leadership. Examples include academic institutions, think tanks, trade associations, nonprofits and even political advocacy groups. While these organizations may not compete directly with your services, they may compete with you in the intellectual or thought-leadership space.

Of course, if you are advocating societal-level changes, as Kimberly Ellison-Taylor and Carl Elefante do, your indirect competitors may be critical to your mission. Make the effort to understand this group of indirect competitors as they may become important allies and referral sources.

TRACKING YOUR COMPETITORS

When it comes to competitors, Visible Experts can put them into two camps. In the first camp are individual experts and firms that both directly compete with you for business and consider you a threat to their success. These traditional competitors have little interest in your business' well being (unless they want to acquire you). It's useful to study your most frequent competitors for one important reason: so you can take steps to differentiate your practice and brand from theirs. Most professional services look similar, at least on the surface. So the more you can distinguish yourself—through the services you offer, the clarity of your focus and your thought leadership—the more likely buyers will notice and remember you. In the second camp are competitors that may compete with you, but who have good reasons to collaborate with you, too. These competitors deserve far more of your attention.

> WHY DO YOUR VERY BEST CLIENTS SELECT YOU RATHER THAN ONE OF YOUR COMPETITORS?

I GET BY WITH A LITTLE HELP FROM MY FRENEMIES

There is a special bond that develops among Visible Experts. Maybe it's their shared experience that arouses respect for other experts. After all, they know what it takes to become an expert. Or maybe it's Visible Experts' love of teaching and mentoring that compels them to help other experts. Whatever the reason, there is clearly something special about their relationship.

Michael Zipursky has found ways to integrate other experts into his firm's service offerings. "We absolutely love working with other Visible Experts. That might mean doing a webinar for a person, and in return they do one for our audience. Sometimes we collaborate on creating content—doing a study or something else along those lines. We also run masterminds and events for our clients. Guest experts will give a talk on their area of Visible Expertise. And we absolutely love that. We think it's critical, because no one person has all the answers. We feel it's very important for our community and the clients that we work with to get those different perspectives, especially from experts in other areas."

Michael is far from alone. Most Visible Experts have stories about other experts helping them at critical junctures in their careers. Rachel Fisch, whom you met in Chapter 2, has learned from some of the best minds in her industry. "What is really interesting is how generous they are with their time and knowledge. It's almost like there is a humility that comes with fantastic expertise."

> RESEARCHING YOUR TARGET AUDIENCE IS ONE OF THE MOST VALUABLE STEPS YOU CAN TAKE TO REVOLUTIONIZE YOUR CAREER.

Rhondalynn Korolak, the expert who takes a contrarian approach to cash management, had a similar experience when she approached a world-renowned expert to review her value-based pricing book. "It is astounding to me that this person, who I held up on a huge pedestal and revered, was so generous with his time and knowledge and support and encouragement. It made a massive difference for me. It took a lot for me to put my hand up and ask because I just presumed that he wasn't going to say anything. But what I have found is that some of the smartest and most visible experts in the world are actually the most generous and the most helpful."

Sometimes, the biggest hurdle to developing relationships with other experts is overcoming your reluctance to reach out. As Rhondalynn explains, "There's a natural tendency for people not to ask those people for help. And those are exactly the people that you *should* ask. These busy people will make time in their day to help somebody that really wants to learn—if you are genuine in your pursuit of becoming better."

Mark Amtower, the expert in marketing to the government, solicits valuable input from fellow experts in a variety of ways. He is part of a group of marketing professionals that meets twice a week. "I'll send people a copy of something that I'm writing—the outline, or maybe the first draft. I get feedback from frontline people and other consultants. It's great. It helps me focus whatever I'm working on and produce something better." Mark also uses mentoring as an opportunity to learn from other experts. "I've started mentoring other government marketing experts. I'll send them a draft of something and say, 'If you have time, give me feedback.' And the feedback I get from them is just extraordinary."

You can learn a great deal from other Visible Experts. Not only can they help you sharpen your subject matter expertise, they can also help you generate new business. As you get to know these frenemy Visible Experts, consider what you can learn from them. Here are just a few things to look out for:

- What are their new ideas? Is there an insight that you can use?
- What issues and topics are they focusing on? Are there any areas where you could collaborate on content?
- Where are they publishing and speaking? Some of these outlets or events might be great opportunities for you.
- Who do they follow on social media? And who follows them? These may be great contacts for you, as well.
- What marketing techniques are they using? You might discover something new.
- What media channels do they own? Perhaps you can appear on their podcast or write guest articles for their blog or newsletter.
- What tools are they using? You may get ideas to make your own process more efficient.

Understanding your competitive space not only helps you differentiate your expertise, it can uncover valuable resources that will propel your career forward, too. From your target audience to your Visible Expert competitors, you have plenty to dig into and learn. But how do you put together a coherent research plan? That's what we tackle next.

HOW TO DO YOUR RESEARCH

Researching your target audience is one of the most valuable steps you can take to revolutionize your career. Below we lay out a five-step process you can follow to guide your own research. If you've never done research before and the whole thing sounds intimidating, don't panic! While it will require some discipline, it doesn't have to be overwhelming. If you take the process one step at a time you will find that research is surprisingly manageable—even fun!

1. **MAKE A LIST OF YOUR AUDIENCES**

   To begin, draw up a list of your target audiences. Audiences can include broad categories (such as prospective clients, amplifiers and referral sources) or cross-sectional audiences (such as different industries or different roles in client organizations). Most aspiring experts will want to research several audiences, and at this stage, don't worry about having too many. On the other hand, trying to research multiple broad and cross-sectional audiences can get hairy quickly. As you work through the process, you will likely end up combining some target audiences and eliminating others.

2. **DRAFT YOUR RESEARCH QUESTIONS**

   Next, consider the range of questions that you want answered. Use the list earlier in this chapter as a starting point. You may even want to turn some of those into groups of related questions. Then think about other questions that will help you and add them to your list.

3. **DECIDE WHAT KIND OF RESEARCH YOU WILL DO**

   Now choose the research approach you want to take. Start with your informal research to generate new ideas to explore. Next do your secondary research, if appropriate, to gain a broad understanding of the marketplace. Then zero in with your primary research. If you are targeting your clients, consider using an objective third party researcher or firm to maintain confidentiality and encourage clients to be candid. This is also

a great time to make note of any ideas for research that would
appeal to your audience and might make good premium content.
If you can repurpose the work you are doing, so much the better!

4. **THINK STRATEGICALLY ABOUT YOUR COMPETITORS**

   Next, look carefully at your competitors in the thought leadership
   space. Who are they? How are you different? What might you
   learn from the more advanced ones? How might they help you?
   What competitive threats do your direct competitors pose?
   What can you learn by studying them? How are you similar
   and different from them?

   As you gather and analyze your
   research, you will want to be looking
   for patterns. These patterns can
   uncover ways to differentiate yourself,
   what is most important to your target
   audiences and how you can help them
   solve their most critical problems.
   This information will tell you what to
   emphasize in your thought leadership.
   And any data you collect about where
   your audiences look for industry
   insights will inform what channels you
   include in your visibility plan.

   > YOU ARE TRYING
   > TO UNDERSTAND
   > HOW YOUR
   > CLIENTS ARE
   > THINKING
   > AND BEHAVING
   > AS A GROUP.

5. **CONDUCT YOUR RESEARCH**

   Exactly how you will conduct your research will depend on the
   type of research you end up doing. And your decision whether
   to do it yourself, collaborate with others at your firm or engage
   a qualified third-party to do it for you can dramatically affect
   how much effort and time you spend. If you will be doing primary
   research, you will need to decide whether to use a standard
   survey (usually online) or interviews, or both. Once you make
   that decision, contact your research subjects and invite them
   to participate. Then you or a researcher can administer the
   survey or conduct the interviews.

If you decide to include a survey in your research, you have a bevy of options to choose from. At the high end are pricey, sophisticated platforms like Qualtrics, which you should only consider if you have considerable research experience. If you are a beginner, try a simpler tool like SurveyMonkey, SurveySparrow or Zoho Survey.

Once you have collected the data you still need to make sense of it. If you have hired an outside researcher, they will usually do the analysis for you. If you are doing it yourself, put all the data into a spreadsheet, then group the responses by question or theme. Read the verbatim responses and look for broad patterns. Don't ignore one-off or outlier answers—sometimes they provide sharp insights—but don't put too much stock in what any one person says, either. Remember, you are trying to understand how your clients are thinking and behaving as a group. That's where you will uncover the greatest insights.

SHOULD YOU DO THE RESEARCH YOURSELF?

In this chapter, you met Dan Adams and Michael Zipursky, both of whom use research to keep abreast of their clients' changing needs and provide an abundance of material for their content marketing machines. Some of Dan's research involved asking clients about his firm's work, so it made sense to use a third-party research firm to ensure the objectivity of the results. But both Dan and Michael also routinely conduct research in-house because they have those skill sets in their firms. Even if you are a solo expert with no research experience, however, there are still practical ways to use research to gain insight into your market and create valuable content.

Research design and data analysis are disciplines all their own, and it's not in the scope of this book to delve into formal research methods. If you can't work with a research firm, you can still gather useful information, however. If you don't have time to learn the fundamentals of market research but can afford to hire an expert to design, deliver and analyze a study, by all means do it. You'll get incredible value from the research process. But if you can't, don't worry about it. Do your best. Enjoy learning some new skills. And try to avoid introducing personal bias into the questions you ask and the conclusions you draw at the end. You are bound to discover many things you didn't know about your clients—which you can use to equip yourself for your Visible Expert journey.

REVISIT YOUR EXPERT PROFILE

In the last chapter, we walked you through the process of drafting your expert profile. Once you have researched your audience and competitors, it's time to pull that draft out of the drawer and give it a good, hard read again. Have you learned anything about your marketplace that would change the way you describe yourself?

As you may recall, your profile should address three issues:
1. **what you do**
2. **who you serve**
3. **the primary benefit you provide**

As you review your initial draft, ask yourself the following questions:

- Is what I do different enough from what my competitors do? If not, is there a different angle I can take? Am I addressing my audience's biggest relevant challenges?
- Have I identified the right audiences? Is there anything I've learned about them that might change the way I describe them?
- Did anything surface in the research that might be an important point of differentiation—or even help define me?
- Does my expert profile make me sound interesting and compelling? If it falls a little flat, is there anything of substance I can add to give it more juice?

You may decide that your expert profile is good as you wrote it. That's great—you nailed it! Or you may need to spend some time changing or adding details. You may decide to rewrite it entirely. All of these are common situations, so don't fret if you feel a little uncertain at this point. Keep working at it until you think you've got it about right. It doesn't have to be perfect. In fact, it's probably going to evolve over time. In the next chapter, you will have another opportunity to revise it.

» Research gives you valuable insight into your target audiences and how they select experts.

» Research can provide a wealth of high-value content for your thought leadership marketing program. It consists of five steps.

» The first step in the research process is selecting your target audiences. Clients and prospects, referral sources, amplifiers, analysts, investors and the general public are some common audiences.

» Second, identify the questions you are trying to answer. We provide a number of questions to get you started.

» Third, determine the kind of research you will do. There are three basic ways to gather research data, which you can use to address almost any question. These are primary research, secondary research and informal research.

» Fourth, identify your competitors and determine how you might learn from them. Competitors in the thought leadership space can also be valuable allies. For example, they can provide support, skill development, market intelligence and referrals.

» Finally, conduct the research. You can take on the research yourself or, if you don't have the time or skills in-house, you can hire a third-party research organization to do it for you.

CHAPTER FOUR

DEVELOP YOUR VISIBILITY PLAN

WHAT IS THE BEST WAY TO BECOME A VISIBLE EXPERT?

Michael Zipursky has some advice. "If you want to become a Visible Expert, number one, get very clear on who you want to serve and what you want to be known for." These may sound familiar. In Chapters 2 and 3, we discussed selecting your target audiences and your expert niche.

"Once you've decided that," he continues, "the next thing would be to start creating your own intellectual property, your own content. Take your ideas, experiences, stories and your expertise and put it out into the world." What Michael is referring to is what we call selecting your issues and topics—the themes and opinions you will become known for and which you will write and speak about frequently. We'll explore this concept in detail later in this chapter.

"Whatever medium you choose, be sure it's one that your ideal clients are actually using," says Michael. "Find a channel or format that you enjoy—one that your ideal clients and those that you want to serve are also consuming. If your clients listen to podcasts, for example, then podcasts may be a great direction for you to go. And then just start putting out content. Start creating. And don't worry about getting things just right. The more that you do this, the easier and more comfortable it's going to become."

What Michael is describing is the essence of a visibility plan. A visibility plan allows you to organize everything you need to do in your pursuit of Visible Expertise, identify priorities and stay on track. In this chapter, we explain how to develop your own visibility plan, including what issues and topics you will focus on and which communication channels you will use to reach your target audiences.

COMPONENTS OF A VISIBILITY PLAN

Your visibility plan has three basic components. The first is your **strategy**. Your strategy should answer questions like these: How will you position yourself in the marketplace? What issues and topics will you "own"? What business challenges do you want to be known for solving?

The second component of your visibility plan is which **techniques** you will use to reach your target audience. Each technique falls into one of three categories: writing, speaking or networking. We will look at these categories in more detail later in this chapter.

The third component is the **frequency** with which you will use these techniques. How often will you give speeches or appear on podcasts? How frequently will you publish blog posts? By documenting your schedule up front, you can monitor the pace of your progress, track your activities and hold yourself accountable.

BUILD YOUR PLAN

START WITH STRATEGY

Every visibility plan begins with strategy. In Chapter 2, we discussed the importance of finding your niche, one that is large enough to support your aspirations yet narrow enough to give you a specialist's competitive advantage. You may already have a clear area of specialized expertise. Or you may still be trying to decide what it should be. If you are in the second category, take a hard look at your audience and marketplace. Did your research uncover any specific opportunities to serve your audience? Can you identify any underserved markets or client needs? Is there a specific industry or service offering that you can focus on? Is there an issue or approach you can "own"?

Besides looking at the opportunities in the marketplace, you should also consider your personality and intellectual style. Are you a natural Bridge Builder who is inclined to connect two different subjects? Or are you a networker who loves to gather best practices and share them? Perhaps you are a Contrarian who holds an unconventional view on some aspect of your industry. Your expertise style can inform your niche and help you determine how you will share your expertise with the world.

In Chapter 3, we explained how to use research to explore your target audiences and competitive environment. With a clear-eyed understanding of your marketplace you can identify what makes you different from other experts and position yourself to address something your audience truly needs, while avoiding the competitive pressures of an overserved market.

IDENTIFY YOUR DIFFERENTIATORS

To attract the attention of today's buyers, being good at what you do isn't enough. You need one or more attributes that set you apart from other experts—something you can point to and say "this is what makes me special." Now, if talking about yourself this way makes you uncomfortable, let us set your mind at ease. Differentiation is not bragging. In fact, it plays an important role in the marketplace. Without differentiation, buyers would struggle to pick one expert over another. By pointing out everything that makes you different, you make the buyer's job easier. And isn't that a big reason you wanted to become a Visible Expert in the first place—to make it easy for clients to choose you?

You can look for your differentiators in a number of places. Start by asking yourself a few questions:

- **Do you specialize in an industry?** If so, it might be a great differentiator. Depending on how many other experts specialize in it, however, an industry focus may or may not be enough on its own. At the very least, an industry focus separates you from the scores of generalists out there, and it can serve as the foundation of your positioning.
- **Do you specialize in a specific service or narrowly defined problem?** Clients often seek out, and are willing to pay more for, expertise in the specific service they need or problem they have. They assume—with good reason—that a specialist will be able to address their issue more quickly and with less risk than a generalist.
- **Do you have a unique business model or approach to solving problems?** We'll expand on this in a moment, but most

"proprietary processes" are not unique enough to rise to the level of a differentiator. If yours truly breaks new ground, however, it may be something to make hay about.

Next, turn to your primary research if you have it. Read through it carefully, paying particular attention to any areas your clients identified as your strengths. Also look out for places where your skill set and your clients' needs converge. Here are a few things to think about as you review the findings:

Do you directly address any of your clients' top business challenges?

- What do your clients think makes you different?
- Why did your clients choose you over someone else?
- What is the biggest value you bring to your clients?
- Were there any surprises in your research findings?

Finally, turn to your competitive research and look at what your top rivals are saying about themselves:

- How do they describe themselves? What is their unique selling proposition, if any?
- What services do they offer?
- Who do they serve? Do they specialize in an industry or service?
- Are they thought leaders? Do they regularly publish or do public speaking?
- How are you different from them? How are you similar?

As you go through the research and ask yourself these questions, keep a running list of potential differentiators. Don't worry about vetting them now—you'll do that next. Just jot down anything that sounds like it might distinguish you from some or all of your competitors.

EVALUATE YOUR LIST
It's time to take a good, hard look at your initial list. You may have fifteen items, or just two or three. If your list feels a little skimpy,

don't worry. It's the quality of your differentiators that counts. Every item on your list must pass these three tests:

1. **Is it true?** Can you deliver on your promise?
2. **Is it relevant to your target audience?** In other words, is it an actual selection criterion?
3. **Is it provable?** Can you support it with believable evidence?

Look at your list again and ask yourself a few questions:

- Could many of your competitors credibly claim the same thing? If you answer yes, then you probably don't have a true differentiator. You don't need to be completely unique. But by the same token, if most of your potential competitors can make the same claim it is probably not going to be a useful differentiator.
- Do you say you have a proprietary process? Again, probably not a differentiator—unless your process really is different. Most experts' processes, however, don't meet that standard. Be brutally honest with yourself, here. Is it just industry best practices dressed up in fancy new language? What about your process is so unusual? If the answer isn't perfectly obvious, your process probably isn't that compelling (which, to be clear, doesn't mean it isn't effective).
- Do you claim better service than your competitors? Good luck getting anyone to buy it, unless you have a trustworthy, unbiased third-party endorsement (such as a J.D. Power award).

How many differentiators should you have? Most experts end up with a list of two to five differentiators, although usually only one (or occasionally, two) is a truly differentiating, defining characteristic. If your list is longer, look at each item critically. Remove any items that simply describe what you do—unless, of course, they are truly unique. The goal is to make this list as tight as possible.

Once you have finished this exercise, go back once more to the expert profile you drafted earlier. Are there any differentiators on your list that belong in that statement? Update your profile to reflect anything important you have learned.

Next, let's turn to the part of your strategy that relates to the issues and topics you will talk and write about.

ADD ISSUES AND TOPICS TO YOUR STRATEGY

What Are Issues and Topics?

One of the most important ways Visible Experts build their reputation is by writing and speaking about a few key ideas. Just as specialization makes your expertise more powerful, focusing your thought leadership on one, two or three areas makes it far more likely you will be remembered for something. We call these areas your "issues." And all of the individual blog posts and webinars and speeches that roll up under each issue we call "topics" (see Figure 4.1).

An issue is a broad subject that is fairly complex and has no simple answer. An example of an issue might be equity in the workplace. Other examples of issues include *optimizing sustainability and finding new ways to finance fledgling enterprises*. Your issues should be broad enough that you can think up countless angles to talk about them. At the same time, they should not have easy solutions, and they should be of great interest to your target audience. In addition, they should be relevant to the kind of services you provide. After all, your ultimate goal is to attract potential clients.

Most experts are known for having expertise in a relatively small number of issues. Most people can handle no more than one or two issues. Mastering three or more can be challenging, and covering a wide range of issues can dilute your focus, anyway. By keeping your range of issues limited, you make it more likely that you will become known for one or more of them.

Large and complex organizations, however, may have more overall issues. Three to five is typical, and some of them may need to be a bit broader to address the concerns of diverse target audiences. It's important to have at least one issue that is relevant to each of a firm's major practice areas. Fortunately, multiple practices can usually share one or more issues.

Topics, on the other hand, are more specific and smaller in scope. A topic might be something you cover in a webinar or a blog post. Think of a topic as the title of something you will write or deliver orally. If one of your issues was "The Future of ERP in Manufacturing," an example of a topic might be *3 ERP Innovations that Will Revolutionize Manufacturing*. If an issue were "How to Manage a Business in Transition," you could write a blog post titled *A Succession Planning Checklist*. You should be able to produce dozens—even hundreds—of topics under each issue.

Thinking about issues and topics in this way allows you to plan ahead. Once you have a handle on your issues, you can build out a detailed calendar of topics weeks or even months in advance.

» How Issues and Topics Work

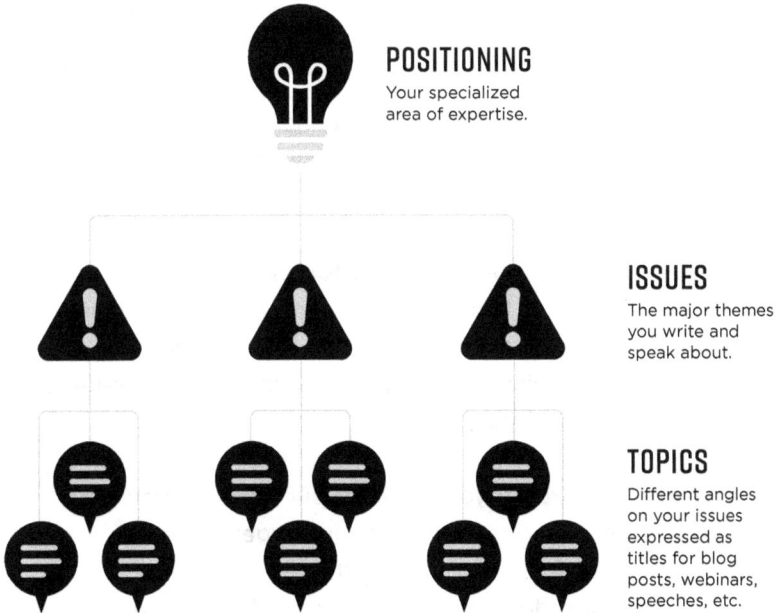

FIGURE 4.1

POSITIONING
Your specialized area of expertise.

ISSUES
The major themes you write and speak about.

TOPICS
Different angles on your issues expressed as titles for blog posts, webinars, speeches, etc.

How Experts Use Issues and Topics

Remember Carl Elefante, the architect who focuses on the issue of sustainability and the built environment? This is a very broad issue that has no simple solutions. It offers many opportunities for Carl to apply his evolving expertise.

When Carl gives a presentation about the need to educate architects to meet the challenges of the future, that is an example of a specific topic. If he were to write an article about how historic preservation is an act of sustainability, that would be another topic that addresses the same issue.

Kimberly Ellison-Taylor is an expert in using technology to solve accounting-related challenges. Or as she describes it, she operates at the intersection of accounting and technology. This issue lends itself to countless topics. Another issue of great importance to her is equity and inclusion in the workplace. Here again, she has a great deal of raw material to turn into specific blog posts and speeches.

In summary, issues are broad in concept and few in number. Topics are more specific and numerous but directly relate to one of your focus issues.

How to Generate Ideas for Issues and Topics

Deciding what issues to focus on, then what topics to write and speak about, may seem difficult at first. It doesn't need to be. Use the four techniques below to help you generate ideas for issues and topics for your visibility plan.

1. **Mine your research.** If you've done your research, you will already have a very good idea of your target audiences' top concerns. What are the big issues they are struggling with? What challenges do they anticipate in the future? What topics capture their attention? Digging into your research is probably the best single way for you to uncover the issues that are best for you. If you are able to do ongoing research, that can help you generate a flow of topic ideas, as well.

2. **Competitor research.** Dive into the research you did on your expert competitors. These are the people or firms that compete for the thought leadership space you are attempting to occupy. They may be either direct competitors, if they also offer competitive services, or indirect competitors, if they generate thought leadership content but do not compete with your services. Are there obvious gaps in the issues covered by other experts? What unique perspective might you have that's not already represented in the marketplace of ideas? Does their content suggest new topics that you should explore? Don't hesitate to talk with other experts and follow their work—their interests may inspire new ideas for issues and topics.

> IT'S IMPORTANT TO HAVE AT LEAST ONE ISSUE THAT IS RELEVANT TO EACH OF A FIRM'S MAJOR PRACTICE AREAS.

3. **Social listening and networking.** Use the power of social media to identify the key issues facing your target industries. What questions are being asked that don't have good answers? Social listening and social networking are particularly helpful techniques to identify emerging and fast-moving topics. Challenges like these tend to surface first on social media because Twitter, Facebook, LinkedIn and similar platforms can reach people in near-real time. Be aware of the language people use to describe these problems. It may give you clues about how to articulate your topics. The same goes for harvesting insights from traditional face-to-face networking and your own clients.

   There is a wide selection of social listening tools on the market at a range of price points. At the time of this writing, popular platforms include Brandwatch, BuzzSumo, Meltwater, Mention and Zoho Social—and this just scratches the surface.

Mark Amtower, a leading Visible Expert in the marketing-to-the-government niche, captures the spirit of this kind of ongoing learning. "I love interacting with pretty much anybody in our market because I learn from every call, every Zoom, every conference, every coffee. So, stay open and learn. Learning to listen was probably my biggest insight because my mouth runs a lot. So learn to listen, understand and address the concerns of those who are sharing with you." If you keep your eyes and ears open to emerging issues and trends you should be able to produce a steady stream of relevant and engaging content.

4. **Keyword research.** If writing online content will be a major part of your plan, keyword research can be a powerful tool in your quest to attract web visitors. Keyword research is especially helpful any time you write topic titles for searchable content such as blog posts, guest articles and videos. There are many keyword research tools available. For example, Google's Search Console and Ubersuggest are good free resources, but a wide range of paid options with more features are available, too, such as Moz, Ahrefs and Semrush. If you are not familiar with these tools and if you don't want to invest the time to learn, you may want to work with a search engine optimization professional to help you attract more readers to your content.

These four techniques should help you generate a wealth of great ideas for issues and topics. Chances are, you will produce more than you can use. How do you narrow the list to the specific issues you will "own" and the topics you will write and speak about?

NARROW YOUR LIST

When evaluating potential issues it's important to consider your personal preferences. No one should have to spend their days working on an issue they have no interest in. But keep in mind that your personal interests are only part of the story. Also consider which issues will be valuable to your clients and help you build your visibility.

FIGURE 4.2

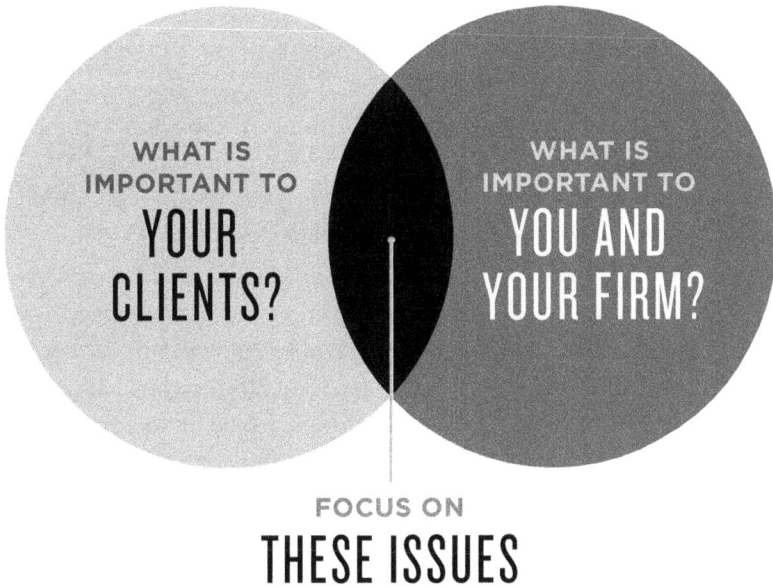

FOCUS ON
THESE ISSUES

We find it helpful to think about this situation as a Venn diagram (Figure 4.2). The left side of the diagram represents all the high priority issues that your target audiences care about. There will be many of them. Most individuals would struggle to become experts in more than one or two major issues even though their firm's services may be relevant to many issues. The right side of the diagram represents the things that you can help clients with. Think of these as the problems that your services and expertise can solve. What issues are you particularly good at helping clients solve? What issues are you most interested in solving? Does the nature of your services give you a competitive advantage in some issues more than others?

You will discover that there is a small but important area where the issues your clients care about and those you're interested in and able to solve overlap. These are the issues you should focus on. Some experts get overwhelmed trying to keep up with the multitude of issues their clients care about. Do not attempt this yourself. Instead, focus on that area of intersection. Your job will be a whole lot easier.

Issues are not forever. Revisit this analysis from time to time to determine if you need to drop an issue or add a new one. You may find that you no longer have a competitive advantage in a particular issue. Remember, being a thought leader means the industry follows, so eventually your original thinking gets adopted by others, including your direct competitors. That may signal that it's time to move on to a new issue.

For each of the issues you identify, follow the same basic process of comparing what topics interest your clients to the topics that are most advantageous for you and your firm. Of course, topics are more variable and will often differ from one audience to another, so you will have many more topics than you have issues. As you get started, you may want to identify five to ten topics for each audience for a given issue. Think of topics as smaller and shorter-term investments. In some cases, you may write or speak about a topic only once or twice. Other topics may come up again and again, recycled or addressed from different angles in blog posts, social media posts, podcasts and speeches. Still other topics may be timely, addressing recent events or short-lived trends. But don't just think small. Many of the best topics address big, evergreen ideas that you can build your reputation upon.

As you consider what topics to write or speak about, use a similar evaluation process as before: determine if each topic candidate fits with your audience's needs and whether it reflects the services you provide.

Let's look at one last example. Let's say your firm helps companies implement their digital transformations. And suppose your research indicates that businesses are no longer asking whether they should invest in a digital transition, but how to do it successfully, instead. You also learn that companies are facing multiple talent challenges, and that many of the transformations they have attempted in the past failed. The reasons they failed revolve around not having qualified talent to lead the transformation. At the same time, your research shows that using outside resources, such as your firm, greatly increases the likelihood of a successful digital transition.

In this example, you might consider adopting an issue like "How to improve the success of a digital transformation." You could then develop topics that are relevant to your audience's specific questions around this issue. For instance, "How to lead your business digital transformation." In the resulting article or speech, you might explore different solutions to the problem and cite the data from your research about how using an outside partner leads to the greatest likelihood of success.

Another topic could be "How to achieve leadership buy-in for your digital transformation." Yet another might be "Two digital transformation strategies: pilot project vs. organization-wide rollout." Keep in mind that topics can have different audiences. If you were speaking to an audience of CEO's and top executives, you might focus on return on investment and the risk profile of different approaches. If, however, you were addressing an audience of implementers, you might focus on the topic of persuading management to staff the project appropriately.

One final note: if you are writing a blog post or online article, your keyword research will inform how you write the title and, to a lesser extent, how you structure the article's content to make sure it receives maximum visibility.

WHAT ARE THE BEST CHANNELS TO REACH YOUR AUDIENCE?
Once you have decided what issues and topics you'll be writing or speaking about, your next decision is which channels you'll use to reach your audience. The best answer is also the obvious one: use the channels that your target audiences use. Or as the old expression goes, "Fish where the fish are."

Of course, if you deliver your content on a channel that your prospects rarely use, it's unlikely to be successful. You will remain stubbornly invisible. The problem is, you may not know where your prospective clients get their information, either online or in the physical world. That's why researching your audience can be so valuable. Refer to the sections in which you ask clients where they look for insights and advice on important business issues. The channels they mention most frequently are usually a great place to start. After all, this is exactly what you will be producing—insights that address your audience's most important challenges.

What do you do if you don't have information on a particular target audience? Look around for secondary research on that audience that covers their preferred channels. Hinge, for instance, publishes research on where clients of Visible Experts look for business-related insights, education and help. We show the results in Figure 4.3.

FIGURE 4.3

» How Buyers Search for Work-Related Topics

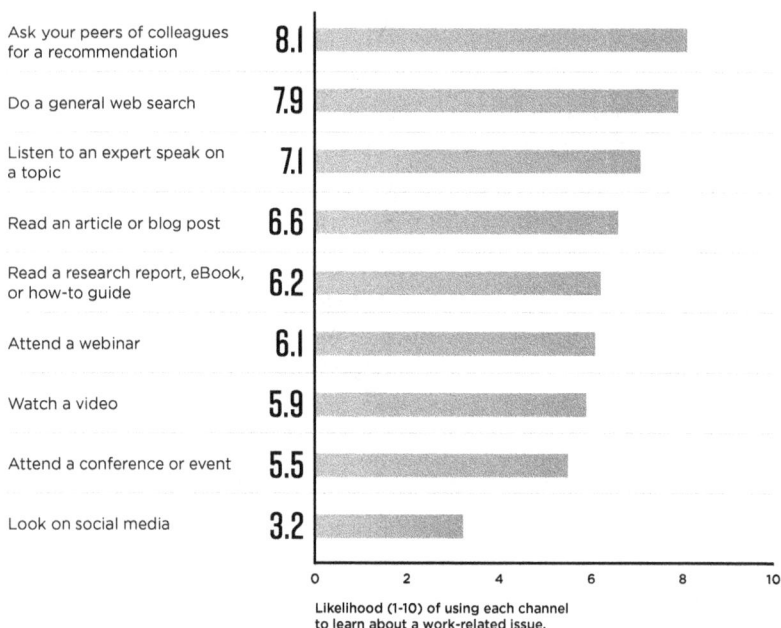

Channel	Likelihood
Ask your peers of colleagues for a recommendation	8.1
Do a general web search	7.9
Listen to an expert speak on a topic	7.1
Read an article or blog post	6.6
Read a research report, eBook, or how-to guide	6.2
Attend a webinar	6.1
Watch a video	5.9
Attend a conference or event	5.5
Look on social media	3.2

Likelihood (1-10) of using each channel to learn about a work-related issue.

Asking for referrals and recommendations is many buyers' first choice when they need to find work-related information. Of course, if you want to benefit from this channel, the people who make the referrals and recommendations either must have direct experience with you or learn about you through another channel.

The second most frequent approach—and only by a whisker—is to use a search engine. This is why SEO is such a powerful way to build your visibility. After that comes an assortment of content formats: listening to speeches; reading articles and blog posts; and consulting research reports, ebooks and guides. With the exception of listening to an expert (unless the audio is also transcribed for readers), these types of content are often searchable online, so SEO is an important consideration when writing for these channels.

Watching webinars and videos come next. These are two digital techniques that take advantage of an expert's live presentation skills. At the bottom of the list are a handful of networking channels, such as attending conferences and events and turning to social media.

If you do not have specific input on the channels your audience prefers, this list is a good place to start as you consider which techniques to include in your visibility plan.

LEAN INTO YOUR SKILLS AND INTERESTS
When selecting a technique be sure to take your personal strengths, preferences and skills into account. If you enjoy public speaking, you may want to pursue that interest further: consider adding techniques that involve oral communication—such as live events, webinars or podcasts—to your plan. If, on the other hand, you have a talent for writing, add a number of those techniques to your repertoire. If you are a good networker, you have a few in-person and digital options to choose from. If you are able to incorporate techniques from each of these realms, so much the better—but it's okay if you prefer to stick to one swim lane at first. You can always learn and add new skills later.

Understanding where your personal interests and skill levels stand today will help you determine which channels to include in your visibility plan. Just keep in mind that there's little benefit in investing time and energy in a channel that your audience will ignore. Personal preference, while an important factor in narrowing your choices, should never override the behavior of your target audiences.

Kimberly Ellison-Taylor not only relies on the techniques she enjoys the most, but she ventures outside of her comfort zone to address the preferences of her audiences. "I have a technical writing minor. I love to write." But she recognizes that her audiences aren't reading all the time. Many watch videos, attend conference presentations, listen to podcasts and attend webinars. "So, I use various communication channels to reach different audiences because different audiences might move across each one of those channels." This strategy works well for Kimberly because she has a very diverse audience and has learned to work in different formats. But it's okay to limit your communication channels—as long as you work with platforms and formats that your audiences use.

One more consideration: Make sure you include techniques that cover all phases of your marketing funnel (see sidebar). In other words, will the techniques you select help you 1) attract new prospects, 2) nurture them and 3) convert them into clients? And will the choices you make equip you to address the major business development challenges you face? Let's explore these issues in more detail.

The Marketing Funnel

STAGE 1:
BEING FOUND

- Digital Ads
- SEO
- Social Media
- Blogging
- Guest Blogging
- Video Blogging
- Speaking & Networking at Events
- Industry Awards
- Marketing Videos

STAGE 2:
ESTABLISHING TRUST & BUILDING RELATIONSHIPS

- Executive Guides
- Original Research
- License Secondary Research
- Email Marketing
- Webinars
- Nurture Calling
- Books

STAGE 3:
CLOSING THE SALE

- Case Stories
- Marketing Collateral
- Free Consultations
- Demos

Your visibility plan is designed to take prospects through the three stages of the marketing funnel. In Stage 1 in the illustration above, you cast your net wide to get in front of as many potential future clients as possible. You will use techniques such as blogging, SEO and social media to maximize your exposure. In Stage 2, you nurture your prospects with more thought leadership materials—some of which may be longer and explore a topic in more depth. This is how you turn people who have a casual interest in you and your expertise into loyal fans. Finally, in Stage 3, you provide opportunities for fans who recognize they can't solve a business problem on their own, as well as anyone else who is ready to buy services like yours, to reach out to you and become paying clients.

YOUR THREE MAJOR CHALLENGES

During your Visible Expert journey, you will need to overcome three major business development hurdles. As you consider which communication channels to incorporate into your plan, keep in mind that it will likely require more than one—and likely several—to address them all.

CHALLENGE 1:
YOU NEED TO BE FOUND

People need to know you exist, what you do and who you do it for. That means you need to be visible to your target audience. To address this challenge, you'll need to clearly define who you serve and how you help them. You will then need to choose techniques that increase your visibility and help people who have never heard of you before discover you.

CHALLENGE 2:
YOU NEED TO DEVELOP TRUST AND ENGAGEMENT

Once people know you exist and have a basic understanding of your expertise, the next major challenge is earning their trust and getting them to engage with you or your content. You develop trust by producing a consistent supply of valuable content and interacting with your followers over time. To achieve these ends, you will need to select techniques that are known to build trust over time.

CHALLENGE 3:
YOU NEED TO CLOSE THE SALE

The final stage in marketing and business development is closing the sale. But do you have the credibility to turn a prospect into a new client? Once again, the communication channels you use, the content you share and the trust you build can dramatically streamline this task.

HOW MUCH EFFORT
CAN YOU AFFORD TO EXPEND?

It's one thing to select a bunch of communication techniques and quite another to use them consistently and effectively. How much implementation time should you build into your visibility plan? This is not a simple question, and the answer will vary from person to person depending on their circumstances. How much effort will you be able to devote to improving your visibility? Is business development your responsibility alone? Or is it something you share with others that only takes a few hours of your time per week?

One way to approach this problem is to reduce it to its simplest form. What is the minimal level of effort it would take to execute a very basic visibility plan? For most experts, this would be about half a day per week. At this stripped-down level, you would need to limit the number of techniques you employ to just one or two key channels. If you are able to put more effort into the plan, however, you will find that success comes more quickly. Putting in one full day per week is probably the next threshold. At this level of investment, you should be able to increase the number of communications channels to three or four.

If you are able to spend more than one full day per week on marketing activities, you should be able to build your visibility and reputation at the highest level. You should be able to manage six or more communication techniques. In fact, the Visible Experts who participated in our study employ an average of 6.5 techniques.

Next, let's look at the specific channel options that are available to you. We'll also see how real-world experts—people who are little different from you—use them to build visibility and trust.

SELECT YOUR COMMUNICATION CHANNELS

Let's review. So far, we've covered many of the foundational elements of your visibility plan. We have discussed how you would like to be positioned in the marketplace. And we have explored the issues and topics that you will become known for. Now it's time to choose which communication channels you will use. Each falls into one of three categories: writing, speaking and networking. But before we dive into those, let's peek into one expert's plan so you can see how specific techniques are used in the real world.

ALMOST IMMEDIATELY WE SAW PERFORMANCE GOING UP

How do your channel choices come together as a plan? Let's return to Dan Adams. Dan, you may recall, is the CEO of The AIM Institute, a firm that helps large organizations improve their product development processes. Here's how he describes his journey toward AIM's current visibility plan: "We determined we wanted to be more visible, so we asked ourselves, 'Now, what do we actually do?' I had written a book a number of years ago. I didn't really promote it strongly, but I found it to be very, very valuable—not because everybody who was coming to our website was going to download the book and read it, but because it gave me a certain level of credibility. I looked at the book as a foundation that was very valuable." From Dan's perspective, the book allowed him to establish trust and credibility.

But what about building visibility in the marketplace? "The first thing we had to do was get our website in order. I remember talking to an expert in this area and she said, 'You know, it's fine that you want to do all these different promotional campaigns, but what are people going to do when they come to your website if the website doesn't make you look good?' And I said, 'Oh, yeah. That's a good point.' So we did a total redesign.

"We didn't do it ourselves. We got professional help. And almost immediately we saw performance going up. Then as we pursued search engine optimization, it just kept going up. Over less than two years, our website performance has seen a fivefold increase in traffic." As impressive as these increases are, Dan recognized the need to engage and nurture his prospects.

"Our particular client base is really busy, so it was important to get our message out on a regular basis—one that was content-rich and would be seen as valuable. We publish a newsletter every month. It's not about us. Instead, each issue is about something we think is really going to be helpful for our clients. We also post a weekly blog called *Awkward Realities* where we try to expose something that doesn't necessarily make a lot of sense. It's very, very short. We publish it every Friday morning so our clients and prospects can read it while they sip their coffee. But the real purpose of these two tools isn't just to wow them. When they are ready to hire us, they're going to go, 'Oh, yeah. I remember. AIM is always sharing this content.' They don't forget us."

In short, Dan and his team use valuable content to establish their expertise, then make sure it's visible when the prospect is ready to buy. As Dan explains, "Content is king. We have about twenty whitepapers, research reports and so forth. We do regular email campaigns to promote those. But our basic push is to get research and content out there that's really valuable, make sure people are reading it and then when they're ready—when their boss says, 'We need to do better voice-of-the-customer work,' or whatever it is— they'll remember us and come to us." Because they have established a high level of familiarity and trust with their prospects, AIM often closes new business with no one else competing for the work. How? They were the clear and obvious choice.

Now that you've seen how Dan Adams' visibility plan plays out, let's explore each of the three communication channel categories and their respective techniques in detail.

WRITING CHANNELS

Writing is probably the most powerful weapon in your visibility arsenal. Not only are there more channel and format options available for writing, it can be applied at every stage of the marketing funnel. In addition, anywhere your writing appears on the web, you can apply SEO techniques to make it visible to the widest possible audience. The act of writing forces you to work through difficult concepts, bringing a discipline and creativity to your thinking that isn't always engaged in other communication categories. Below are several popular writing channels for you to consider. We've included many of the key benefits and best uses for each.

Books and ebooks. There's nothing like a physical book to convey substantial expertise. Writing the definitive book in your niche area of focus is a great way to demonstrate the depth of your expertise, even if many of your prospects never actually read it. Writing a book is a major undertaking that will demand a great deal of your time. And if you use an established publisher, it can take a year or more to hit bookstore shelves once you've finished writing. Self-published books and ebooks enjoy many of the same benefits of traditionally published books, while reducing costs and time to market. Books are excellent tools to increase visibility and establish credibility.

Blogs. Blog posts not only attract visitors to your website but can showcase the range of your expertise, too. When a blog is well optimized for SEO, it also tends to be the most trafficked part of a website. Blog posts are ideal for building top-of-funnel visibility, as well as nurturing existing relationships.

Guest blog posts and articles. Publishing on other people's blogs and in reputable publications is a great way to expand your reach. It can also help spread your name to audiences who don't already know you. In addition, guest posts and online articles can be used to boost your SEO if they include links back to your website (just keep in mind that some publications allow such links, while others do not).

Executive guides and white papers. These longer form pieces of content explore a topic in more depth than a typical blog post, but they are much less work than a book. Executive guides usually target business executives and run approximately 10 to 30 pages in length. They explain a topic at the level of a business executive rather than practitioner and may include easy-to-understand tables and charts. White papers tend to be more technical and are usually written for practitioners and influencers rather than business executives. Guides and white papers can be powerful media to nurture prospects and build confidence in your expertise. If you put them behind a registration form on your website, they can be used to convert web visitors into leads.

Newsletters. Newsletters are a traditional communication channel for nurturing relationships and staying in front of target audiences. Today, most newsletters are digital but they serve the same function as their paper forebears. Newsletters provide a convenient way to keep in touch with your clients and prospects on a regular basis. Follow Dan Adams' lead and focus on content that is practical and educational rather than material that is self-promotional or focused on your firm.

Research reports. Using research as content can be a great way to establish your expertise and increase your credibility. Research is some of the most credible and widely shared content you can produce. Where do you get research to share with your audience? You can either produce your own original research or you can license existing research from a third party to distribute to your audience. Research reports are useful to increase visibility and nurture relationships.

SPEAKING CHANNELS

If you are comfortable in front of crowds, speaking in person or online offers a few advantages that are not available in written content. First, it's more personal. Whether you are speaking to a packed room or an invisible group of webinar attendees, your audience is able to associate a face (or, in the case of podcasts and radio, a voice) with your expertise. That's a powerful connection. Second, your audience gets to sample your thinking and expertise in action. Even though your message is delivered in a controlled environment, that experience is enough to generate feelings of trust. Third, as a presenter you are automatically in a position of authority. Your words, opinions and advice carry more weight than they might in another setting. Fourth, if you are participating in a live event, you can leave time for questions and answers—and address a few of your audience's challenges. Below are some of the most common speaking channels. Most of these can be used to increase visibility and nurture relationships.

Conferences. Speaking at conferences is an effective way to reach a specific audience group. A conference can be both expensive and time consuming, so be sure to seek out events that are well attended by your target audience. Your goal should be to secure speaking opportunities, not just attend the conference. If you can, try to incorporate research data into your presentations to make them more informative and persuasive. Public speaking at conferences is a fantastic way to support your expertise, as well. It can expose you to new audiences as well as deepen your engagement with those who know you.

Webinars. Webinars are today's digital version of speaking engagements and seminars. One of the nice features of a webinar is that you can record the presentation then offer it later on an on-demand basis. This gives your webinars a long shelf life. Webinars are an excellent way to nurture people who already know who you are. At the same time, they can be a powerful tool to impress newcomers, as well. And with the right partnering and promotional strategy, they can also be an excellent way to expand your visibility.

Podcast and radio appearances. While the popularity and reach of traditional broadcast radio may be waning, podcasts have come on strong as a viable channel to share information about business-related topics. They are a great way to increase your visibility and nurture relationships. Podcasts are well suited for experts who are good talkers and interact easily with others. You can either establish your own podcast, as many experts have, or seek out guest appearances on other people's podcasts. However, don't dismiss radio outright. Today, many radio shows are not only broadcast live but recorded and made available to listeners on demand.

Videos and video blog posts. Video is gaining traction as a preferred channel for many people. Video is an ideal medium for experts who are better speakers than writers. Videos can be used in a variety of ways. They can become video blog posts, arranged as channels on video platforms such as YouTube or included in relevant places on your website. Videos are also critical to establishing your speaking credentials. In the next chapter, we'll discuss why a speaking reel is an essential tool to secure speaking engagements. Videos and video blog posts build visibility and nurture relationships.

NETWORKING CHANNELS

Networking was once the second most important business development activity after referrals. Today, it has dropped somewhat in popularity as the internet transformed the way services are bought and sold. Nevertheless, networking remains a very powerful technique to meet new people and build relationships. As we explain below, networking comes in two basic flavors: in-person and social media.

In-person networking. This is the traditional form of networking that we're all familiar with. It involves encountering prospective clients at conferences, networking events and one-on-one meetings and developing relationships with them in person. It is part of almost every Visible Expert's toolkit, and some experts rely on it as a primary business development channel. It is most valuable as a nurturing technique, although it can be of some use to expose you to new prospects.

Social media networking. Social media is the digital version of in-person networking. It can be used as a promotional tool to share content with others and raise your visibility. It is also a powerful way to engage with and nurture individuals. In fact, some experts make social media their primary communications channel. Unlike most of the experts in this book, Jody Padar built most of her reputation as "The Radical CPA" through social media—so she is living proof that social media can be used to achieve exceptional visibility. "A lot of people think social media is really for talking," says Jody, "but like any good conversationalist, most of what happens in social media is listening. I have a large following on social media, so I read, and I listen and then I respond to them. And I think that's probably what most other thought leaders do. They just don't do it in an online world because my thought leadership was born online. It really lives online."

Now that we have explored the major communications channels at your disposal, let's look at a defining feature of another Visible Expert's plan.

IT'S DOING ITS WORK

Michael Zipursky is a great example of a Visible Expert who uses research to build his reputation, deepen his knowledge, uncover the topics his clients are most interested in and supply a wealth of valuable content. You may recall that Michael's firm focuses on helping consulting practices grow and improve their performance.

He explains how the process works. "Some of our surveys explore the area of marketing and business development in consulting. Others look at consultants' fees and pricing strategies. We also have a survey on lifestyle, health and wellness for consultants. All of these surveys help us better understand the market that we want to serve. We get a lot of ideas from those surveys about what kind of content, articles, podcasts, training and new programs we might offer—based on what we're seeing the market wants to learn more about and where they have the greatest needs."

When it comes to turning the research into content, "we don't reach out to ideal clients directly, one-to-one, to say, 'hey, we've done this survey, and let's discuss this.' We don't use it as a business development tool in that way." Instead, the research is fuel for the firm's thought leadership content. "When we compile all the data from the surveys, we create a report or a long-form article explaining the results, along with the graphs and charts." And then comes the critical step of promoting the valuable content they

created. That's where other communication channels swing
into action.

"We then promote the research on our website. We might promote
it on our podcast. We will sometimes run ads to reach more people.
We always put it on social media, and people really appreciate it,
because we see a lot of engagement on those posts. So it's doing
its work in terms of marketing and brand development." Of course,
Michael has assembled a team of people to work on research-driven
content, so they can accomplish a lot. But even if you are in a solo
practice, the same basic approach can work for you. Select the
same channels, just adjust the number of studies and publications
to match your time and resources.

DRAFT YOUR PLAN

Now it's time to pull together everything you've learned and
document your plan. Begin by specifying which target audiences
you want to reach (see Chapter 3). What industries are they in, and
what job positions will you target? Are there other audiences you
should consider, such as referral sources and amplifiers? Next, write
down your expert positioning or niche (see Chapter 2). What are
you an expert in? Do you need to specialize or narrow your focus?
Most likely, you'll rely heavily on the thinking and research we
covered in Chapters 2 and 3 to clarify your area of expertise and
how you are different from your competitors.

Add the issues and topics that you will prioritize as you promote
your expertise (see the section on issues and topics earlier in this
chapter). What key challenges do your clients care about? What
services do you offer? Look for issues where your services and your
clients' challenges overlap. Most individual experts will focus on one
or two issues. Larger organizations with multiple practice areas may
have more issues, usually three to five that they share across the
organization.

Begin drafting a list of topics that you will cover in individual blog
posts, webinars, speeches and other activities. It may be helpful

to format these as titles—you can always tweak or change them later. Remember, some of these titles may need to include keywords, especially those you want to make findable through online search.

Next, identify which communication channels you will use (see the relevant section earlier in this chapter). Start with a clear understanding of which communication channels your clients favor. Also consider which communication channels you are most comfortable with and how much time you can commit to using them. Choose channels in which your preferences and those of your clients overlap.

Finally, consider the level of effort that you will be able to devote to carrying out your overall visibility plan. If you can devote only a few hours per week to implementing your plan, you will use fewer techniques and do them less frequently. If you are able to commit more hours, you can use more techniques and do them more frequently. For example, a low-effort plan may include writing a blog post once a month. A mid-level-effort plan, however, may commit you to blogging once a week. For each communication channel in your plan, specify how often you will use that channel. Try to be as realistic as you can about what you can accomplish in the time you allocate to these activities.

After you have drafted this part of your plan, set it aside for a little while. Come back in a day or two and review it. Have you addressed all three challenges of the business development process? Are you including enough of the right activities to be found by people who don't know you? Do you have a way to nurture those people who know you exist? Do you have the credibility it takes to close the sale? Also consider the overall level of effort. Have you selected enough communication channels? Will you be able to manage the ones you've selected? Are you committing enough of your time to be successful? Once you have reflected on these questions, make any necessary adjustments. But don't worry if you are still not certain. After you begin to implement your visibility plan you can always modify it based on your real-world experiences.

» Your visibility plan has three basic components: 1) strategy and positioning, 2) your communication techniques and 3) the frequency of each technique.

» As part of your strategy, you need to identify a small number of broad issues that you will focus on. You will also begin thinking up specific topics that relate to each issue.

» Next, you will determine which communication channels to employ. You need to balance your target audiences' preferred channels with your own preferences and skills. The channels you select must also address three business development challenges: being found, nurturing the relationship and closing the sale.

» The level of effort you can devote to increasing your visibility will determine how frequently you use each channel.

» Give yourself some time to review your plan and make adjustments.

CHAPTER FIVE

BUILD YOUR VISIBILITY TOOLKIT

IN THE LAST CHAPTER WE FOCUSED ON DEVELOPING YOUR VISIBILITY PLAN. THIS PLAN LAYS OUT YOUR STRATEGY, WHICH COMMUNICATION CHANNELS YOU WILL USE AND HOW OFTEN YOU WILL USE THEM.

In this chapter we're going to introduce some of the most important tools you will need to implement your plan. By tools, we mean infrastructure such as a high performance website and an email marketing system, as well as the marketing materials you will use to promote your expertise, such as professional bios and social media profiles. Each piece is essential to the success of your plan.

An important point to remember is that the tools you will need as a Visible Expert may be different from those used by a traditional subject-matter expert. For example, most Visible Experts will need a press kit and a speaking reel—items that most subject matter experts won't have. Let's examine some of the key tools you will need and how you will tailor them to suit a Visible Expert.

HIGH PERFORMANCE WEBSITE

In the last chapter we learned more about Dan Adams, the Visible Expert who helps large companies improve their product development processes. As you may recall, he explained that after his firm redesigned its website they experienced a 500 percent increase in web traffic. But why is your website so important? We asked Dan for his perspective.

"I go to a lot of websites. On many of them, after five or ten minutes I still don't know what the company does. Maybe they could explain it if you asked them, but they haven't taken that extra step to put it in a form that's accessible on their website." Confusing people is not a winning way to acquire new clients. Dan chose a more productive path. "Our website is all about content, so it's attractive to somebody who wants to learn and build their business over the long-term. In a way, we've set up a self-selection process."

Dan is on to something. A Visible Expert website should clearly describe your areas of expertise, your target clients and how they benefit from working with you. But that's just the beginning. It is also a convenient storehouse and distribution point for your educational content—in fact, it will become the centerpiece of your whole marketing program.

As Dan mentioned, your website should be a place where potential clients can qualify themselves. If you feature content that is highly relevant and useful to your target audience—and if you make your content easy to discover using SEO and other techniques—you are going to attract interested, qualified visitors. Visitors who are more likely to be motivated to buy your services. Conversely, people who don't find your content relevant are unlikely to be attracted to you. That means less time wasted dealing with unqualified leads.

But it gets better. Those website visitors that follow you for an extended period of time can become some of the most qualified leads you ever receive. In our experience, they routinely outperform even the warmest referrals. Often they won't even seek out competing bids. Why? With every blog post they read, every video they watch and every webinar they attend, these prospects' trust in you deepens—to the point that when it comes time to hire someone to solve their business problem they think of you. And in many cases, only of you.

By now, you understand why a website must have a clear and focused message. And you have a general sense that it is a place where your content will be stored and distributed. But what specific features does a high-performance Visible Expert website have? Below are five critical elements you'll need to deliver on your plan.

A blog. A blog is a place where you can publish your original thought leadership content. Most blog posts run from relatively short (500–800 words) to quite long (2,500–5,000 words). Research by HubSpot, Neil Patel and others suggests that longer posts tend to perform better in search engines because they provide ample room to explore a topic in depth. We call these long-form pieces "cornerstone posts," and they can be good anchors for your key issues. You may want to consider including occasional cornerstone posts in your content calendar. The vast majority of your blog posts, however, can be shorter pieces that either dive into a very specific subject or address a topic at a relatively high level. Blog posts will be the best tool you have to attract search engine traffic, so you'll want to optimize each post for one or more appropriate keywords. You can also use your blog to cultivate relationships with other Visible Experts. Just ask them to contribute guest posts to your blog. This is an especially good technique if curating other people's content is a part of your Visible Expert style.

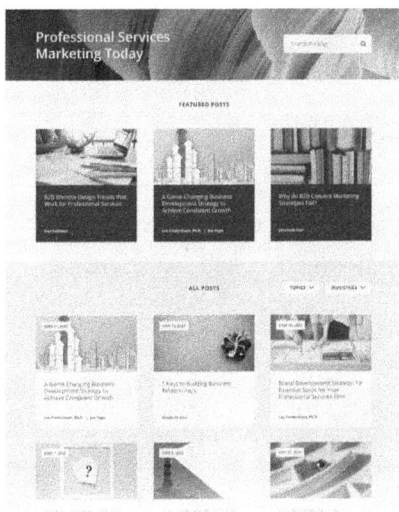

You may be tempted to host your blog on a dedicated blogging platform or on a different URL. Do not do this. Only by hosting the blog on your website's domain (and not a subdomain like blog.yourwebsite.com) will you receive the full benefit of your SEO strategy. Each time a blog post achieves high search rankings it contributes to the overall authority of your website—incrementally making it easier to achieve higher rankings for other posts and web pages.

Downloadable thought leadership. Not all content is created equal. For instance, blog posts—partly because of their length and partly because they are free—are the currency of content marketing. But there is another class of content that dives into a topic at greater depth and is held in even higher esteem by your readers. We call these materials "downloadable thought leadership" or "valuable content." Examples of valuable content include research reports, executive guides, ebooks, white papers, courses and webinar recordings.

Often, this sort of high-value content is housed behind a registration form. Requiring registration not only creates an impression that the material is exclusive, it allows you to capture basic information about the person so you can establish a direct communication channel with them, typically through email. Limit the information you require on the form so that you don't scare valuable prospects away. Of course, do your best to ensure your long-format content delivers the value you promise, and keep any self-promotional language separate from the content itself (for instance, including an ad for your services in your guide or white paper is perfectly okay—as long as it is clearly distinct from the text). Providing this kind of practical educational content encourages people to keep following you. Self-promotional marketing copy, on the other hand, turns people off and encourages people to unsubscribe from your list.

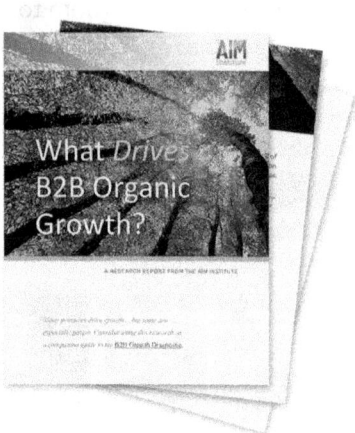

Credentials package. Your credentials package differs from a typical professional bio in several ways. First, it should list or, if practical, link to your current thought leadership content. Second, if public speaking is in your visibility plan, your profile should feature your speaking talents by including a list of past speaking engagements and links to your press kit, speaking profiles, professional photography and speaking reel. Of course, it should also include relevant details about your credentials and accomplishments. We'll explore your credentials package in detail in a moment.

Press kit. A press kit, or media kit, is a document you can provide to a media contact that summarizes key information about you. It describes your expertise and identifies issues and topics that you are qualified to speak and comment on. It usually includes links to samples of your content, as well as professional photography. We'll describe your press kit more fully below.

Offers or calls to action (CTAs). Offers, or CTAs, give prospects an easy way to take a next step in their relationship with you or your content. Offers are most effective when you place them in an appropriate context, whether that's on your website, in your valuable content or anywhere else you want to encourage people to deepen the relationship. For example, an offer for a free consultation would be very appropriate on pages that describe your services. After all, people who are reading about your services are

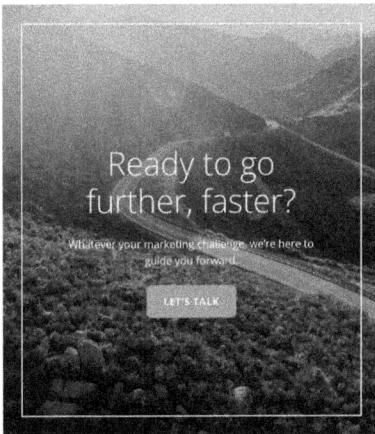
Ready to go further, faster?

Whatever your marketing challenge, we're here to guide you forward.

LET'S TALK

likely looking for a firm like yours, and they may have questions, and a free consultation might be exactly what they need at that moment. Your blog readers, however, probably aren't ready to talk with you. Instead, they are more likely to be interested in downloading valuable content that goes deeper into a subject directly relevant to the post they just read. Your webinar attendees might get excited about a free white paper on the topic, or even a free consultation.

An offer is only going to work if the context is right and you make it crystal clear what your audience should do next.

YOUR CREDENTIALS PACKAGE

In Chapter 2, you learned how to draft your expert profile. While your expert profile captures the essence of your positioning, it is not a substitute for a full bio. In fact, a Visible Expert's bio is different from a traditional professional bio (we'll explain how it's different in a moment). In addition, anytime you solicit a speaking opportunity, podcast interview or similar opportunity, it's convenient to have a portfolio of materials at the ready that provides everything a person needs to understand who you are, evaluate your speaking and writing skills and promote you to their audience. We call this your credentials package.

Below are some typical components of a credentials package, though you can modify it to suit your particular requirements. For instance, if you don't do public speaking, you won't need a speaking reel.

Your expert bio. Your expert bio should focus primarily on your area of expertise. A reader should be able to quickly grasp what you are an expert in. Use your expert profile as a starting place, but you will need to add more material, too. Any background material you include, however, should support your positioning and expert standing. Most traditional bios paint a very broad picture, from the person's education to every type of work experience in their background. A Visible Expert's profile bio tends to be much more focused and specific to their niche. As you consider what to include, ask yourself whether your target audience would consider it important.

Links to recent content. Because Visible Experts generate a lot of thought leadership content, it's important to include links to recent relevant content. This can be a bit of a stumbling block if you are an aspiring Visible Expert who hasn't produced much content yet. That's why one of a Visible Expert's early tasks is to begin establishing a body of work. At first, link to whatever thought leadership writing you have, if any. You can—and should—update your profile bio often as you fill in the gaps and develop new material.

List of awards and accomplishments. Develop a list of any notable awards or accomplishments that you have earned. Awards add third-party credibility to your expertise. Also create a list of your recent or most significant speaking engagements.

Links to social media accounts. Include links to one or more social media accounts. This makes it easy for people to follow you and to learn more about your recent activities.

KARL SPEAKS!

View Karl's speaking reel

WATCH THE REEL ▶

BOOK KARL TODAY

PRESS KIT

Link to speaking reel. A speaking reel is a relatively short piece of video that includes samples of your recent speaking engagements. When someone is considering booking you for a speaking engagement, they can watch the reel and see you in action. Speaking reels are typically two to five minutes in length and usually contain multiple clips of you speaking at different events. If you don't have a variety of material to sample, just include an extended clip of a speech you gave at a single event. If you do public speaking but don't have any video of your work yet, arrange for a videographer to shoot your next event.

Speaker introduction. This is a short blurb that someone introducing you at a speaking event can read to the audience. It gets to the point, and it is often a bit punchier than a traditional bio. This saves your audience the agony of sitting through the introducer reading your entire bio. You may want to include two or three different versions of different lengths.

Bio brief. At times you will be asked to provide a short bio. It might accompany a blog post or article you wrote, or it may be used by a reporter to describe you in a piece of journalism. For these situations, you will want a bio at hand that you can send at a moment's notice. It is not uncommon to have word length limits on bios so having a few options available will save you a lot of time. We recommend you prepare versions of your bio at three different lengths: roughly 250, 100 and 40 words.

Professional photography. Visible Expert credentials packages often include multiple photographs. In addition to traditional headshots, try to include a variety of poses and settings, which can be useful to promote speaking engagements and other activities. Hire a professional to shoot these, if you can, as many venues expect stylish, high-quality photography. Include samples of your photos in your profile, as well as links to download high-resolution files.

Your credentials package is just one part of your promotional package. As your visibility grows, you'll want to put together a press kit, too.

YOUR PRESS KIT

When members of the media look for experts to include in their stories, they need an easy way to understand an expert before they reach out to them. That's where a press kit can make all the difference. A press kit (also called a media kit) supplies all the information and supporting material they need to proceed with confidence. Here are elements you may want to include in your own Visible Expert press kit.

Press contact info. Chances are, this is you. But if you are part of a larger organization, it could be a PR professional or another individual who handles media inquiries. Include a name, email address and phone number.

Expert bio. Include a copy of your full expert bio.

Links to social media accounts. Reporters often check out your social media first. Make it easy for them.

Professional photography. Add some or all of the photos from your credentials package.

List of awards and accomplishments.
Again, you can snatch this from your credentials package. If you deliver a lot of speeches, you may want to break out your speaking engagements into a separate list.

Link to your firm's logo. If you are part of a larger firm, include a link to download a zipped file of your logo in JPG and EPS formats (feel free to include other formats if you have them).

Firm description. If you are part of a larger organization, include a brief description of your firm. Be sure to describe what it does, who it serves and any areas of specialization. Optionally, you may also include when it was founded, what size it is, how many offices it has and similar information.

Client list. This should include only clients you have personally worked with. The more well-known the names on this list, the better. If you work primarily with small clients, you may be better off without this component. It's not likely to catch a reporter's attention and could even be a liability.

Media quotes and mentions. If you have been quoted in the media, include the publication names either in list form (if you have many) or in your expert bio. If you (not your firm) have been mentioned in an article or show, include any clips that present you in a favorable light.

List of speeches, articles and appearances. This can include speeches, podcast and radio appearances, major articles you've published and similar credibility-establishing activities.

SET UP YOUR PROFESSIONAL
SOCIAL MEDIA PROFILES

Social media has evolved significantly over the years. Government contracting marketing expert Mark Amtower has had a front row seat.

"When social networks came in," says Mark, "I had my biggest leap forward. I joined LinkedIn on February 11, 2004, and I started using it seriously in 2007 after I read Jason Alba's book, *I'm on LinkedIn— Now What*. Then I read David Meerman Scott's first edition of *New Rules of Marketing and PR*. David didn't talk about LinkedIn at all, but he talked about the democratization of information using all of these new tools and platforms. So I took what Scott said and applied it to LinkedIn, and I have focused on that for the last fifteen years. LinkedIn is the most powerful marketing tool available in our market, with two-and-a-half million feds on LinkedIn and at least 552 federal agency company pages. You can find little niches of people in there, people you need to reach out to and influence. And most of the market still doesn't get that. I still have a relatively open playing field there because I'm not a LinkedIn generalist. I'm a GovCon LinkedIn specialist."

Social media is an important part of many Visible Experts' visibility plans, so getting it right is a priority. But it can be a bit of a challenge because each platform has its own approach to structuring profiles. Fortunately, there are some common strategies and elements that you can apply to each.

- Use your Visible Expert profile bio as the source material for your profile. Paste it in and edit as you see fit.
- Use a high-quality, professional photo.
- Most platforms also allow you to share your most recent content, so keep that in mind as you invest time and energy in blog posts and other thought leadership pieces.
- Include a list of important awards and accomplishments, as well as your educational background. These help establish credibility.
- Use the recommendations provided by each platform to enhance your profile further.

» Sample Social Media Profile

FIGURE 5.1

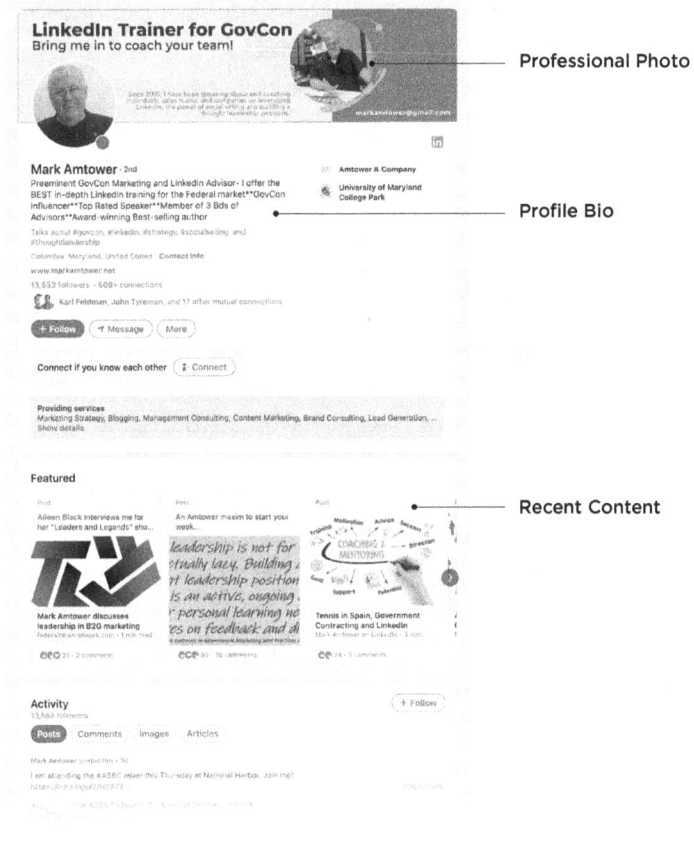

— Professional Photo

LinkedIn Trainer for GovCon
Bring me in to coach your team!

— Profile Bio

— Recent Content

But don't forget, different platforms have different styles, so the approach that works well on one platform may fall flat on another, as Rachel Fisch learned the hard way: "I tried to take the tone I used on Twitter—which is a very authentic, very cheeky Rachel Fisch— and apply that to LinkedIn. I was really surprised at how posts that would take off like wildfire on Twitter would fall flat on LinkedIn. That really drove home how important it is to make sure that you create and deliver content that is appropriate for the platform and your connections on that platform. You can still be authentic and express your more casual side on Twitter while being a little bit more formal and professional on LinkedIn."

EMAIL MARKETING SYSTEM

It's easy to take email for granted. The oldest and most established digital marketing tool of them all, email can feel a little quaint and outmoded. But don't be fooled. Email is still one of the most formidable marketing tools at your disposal. So far, no social media platform or new technology has replaced its power, features and benefits. First, it has near universal reach in the world of professionals and their buyers. If there is one tool everyone uses every day, it's email. Even LinkedIn—the undisputed king of professional services social media platforms—is used only a small fraction as often as email. Second, you can easily personalize emails, even when reaching out to hundreds or thousands of people. Third, emails get far more engagement than social media posts. Nothing else comes even close to their level of performance. Finally, you can track every open, click and conversion with great precision. There is no better channel to communicate with your audience. Let's explore some of the key elements of a successful email strategy.

Select your platform. Modern email marketing can't be done effectively from your Microsoft Outlook or Gmail email browser. Instead, seek out a dedicated email service provider to deliver emails more reliably, automatically handle opt-outs and bounces, and supply the analytics you will need to measure the success of your campaigns. At the low end, tools like MailChimp or Constant Contact provide plenty of power to get you started at an affordable price point. At the high end are sophisticated, feature-rich platforms like HubSpot and Pardot—usually best suited for firms or experts with marketing automation experience. Ask around and do some internet research to find the right tool for you.

Build your list. The most fundamental component of your email strategy is your list. While you may be tempted to take a shortcut and purchase an existing list, that almost never pays off—and it's illegal to use such a list in many states and countries. Purchased lists don't work, anyway, for one good reason: the people on them don't know who you are. The whole purpose of an email list is to build a following of interested fans, people who not only know you but look forward to your next missive. As your list grows larger, some people will inevitably forget who you are or lose interest, but that's okay because you will be continually adding new people to your list.

So how does an email marketing system work?

The easiest way to build your email list is by encouraging people to respond to an offer, often on your website. For instance, a person visits your website, sees an offer that interests them and fills out a form to get access to the thing being offered. The email address they provide in the form then is appended to your list. This kind of list is called a response list. To build a response list, make your content as visible as possible using a combination of techniques, including search engine optimization, posting on other people's blogs, writing articles and conducting webinars. If you can entice people to go to your website and fill out a form, you can build an email list.

As we described above, the key to turning web visitors into contacts on your list is offers. Offers persuade people to exchange personal information for something they want. The most common type of offer is a downloadable piece of premium content, though it could be something else, such as a demo or a free consultation. To ensure you aren't adding unnecessary friction to the transaction and inadvertently depressing your response rate, keep your forms as short as possible. Consider starting with the bare minimum number of fields—name and email address. You can always experiment with requiring more information later. Just keep in mind that the more fields you require, the fewer conversions you will get.

Today's privacy laws and regulations require that people give you explicit permission to engage with them over email. Usually, this involves including a checkbox on your form, which gives their consent to receive more valuable content and offers from you in the future. But don't worry. Your best prospects truly value your expertise and actually want to hear from you. Most Visible Experts find that people are more than willing to exchange a limited amount of information for the opportunity to receive valuable free content from an expert they trust. Of course, it is essential that you deliver on your promise and provide content that is indeed valuable.

Another way to build your email database is by compiling a list of people you've already established a relationship with. You can even include people you meet at networking events and exchange business cards with. Just make a habit of asking if it's okay to add them to your email list. Of course, you don't want to take advantage of anyone. Provide an easy way to opt out of your emails. Fortunately, most email marketing systems automatically include this functionality to comply with privacy regulations.

When to reach out. Don't assume each person that downloads a piece of content is going to be a qualified lead. In most cases they are not. So don't bother reaching out to them individually. Even if you were to require the person to provide an extensive amount of information on your online form in an attempt to qualify them, you would fail. The way most people turn into leads is by nurturing them over time. They will reach out to you or respond to an offer when they are ready to engage.

How often to mail. You may wonder how often you should send emails to your list. There is no perfect answer to that question. In part, it can depend on how much perceived value each mailing delivers. If you are providing a stream of helpful, insightful articles and videos, it's hard to mail too often. Some experts send emails daily and maintain an excellent relationship with people on their list because everything they send provides exceptional value. Keep that lesson in mind, then mail to your list as often as is practical. The tempo of your mailings will be determined by the rate you can develop content. That might be once a week, twice a week or twice a month. Large organizations with multiple Visible Experts might send to their list multiple times a week. If you are an individual expert with limited resources, however, just be careful that you don't send email too infrequently or irregularly. People are more likely to stay engaged if you have a regular flow of insights. Consistency is the key.

Unsubscribes. People will unsubscribe from your list. Make your peace with it now. In fact, unsubscribes are a good thing because they are a way for people who are unlikely to become clients to leave your marketing ecosystem. No harm done. That said, every marketer (and that includes you now) worries about accidentally alienating the right people. So keep an eye on how many people unsubscribe and watch out for spikes. Your email marketing platform provides convenient reporting on this metric. It is possible to mail to your list too often, but only if *what* you send is lacking. The answer is to give away more than you ask for. Offering useful, relevant free content to an audience that wants it will generate relatively few unsubscribes. However, as soon as you ask your audience to buy something or reach out to you directly, you will turn some people off. The more asks you make, the more unsubscribes you will get.

> IT IS POSSIBLE TO MAIL TO YOUR LIST TOO OFTEN, BUT ONLY IF WHAT YOU SEND IS LACKING.

Our rule of thumb, based on years of experience, is to freely give away your expertise at least three to four times as often as you ask for something. That should minimize the number of unsubscribes you receive while still allowing you to deliver the kinds of hard offers that can help turn followers into new business. And any time you ask for something, be sure to point out the benefits of responding to your offer. As you track your unsubscribes over time, you will get a feel for what types of offers drive different levels of unsubscribes.

Automating the system. Today, email marketing can be largely automated. Marketing automation software can even be configured to send emails in response to specific prospect behavior. For instance, you can set up automated emails, or even customized series of timed emails, that are triggered whenever someone responds to one of your offers. This can save you considerable time—and ensure that your responses are timely and engaging. However, marketing automation can get complicated quickly. If you are new to it or don't have a skilled resource to help you, keep things very simple at first. Use it to set up, schedule and send simple emails to your full list. Then as you learn more, consider adding more sophisticated features like nurture sequences, list segmentation and A/B testing.

If it's not already part of your marketing automation software, you will also need CRM software to manage and organize your contact list. Our research has shown that actively using a CRM system is associated with faster growth and higher profitability. So, take advantage of these powerful tools to build, deliver and optimize your email marketing campaign.

This is all great advice if you are a solopreneur or work at a small firm. But what if you are part of a large firm that doesn't have an email marketing system? Or if they do, what if you don't have access to it? At the end of this chapter, we provide a few strategies you can use to work around these constraints.

CONTENT CALENDAR

A content calendar is an essential tool to keep you organized and on track, and it's a critical part of your visibility plan. In your overall plan, you lay out your strategy and how often you will do each activity. Your content calendar takes these decisions to the implementation level. In your calendar, you will plot out every activity—each day of each week of each month. It is a convenient tool for planning your activities, tracking your progress and keeping you honest.

You can create your calendar using whatever tool you like: a physical notebook, an online calendar, a Word document or a spreadsheet. At Hinge, we use a Google Sheet, which every expert in the firm can access.

» Sample Content Calendar

Month	Activity/Title	Type	Due Date	Date Done	Keyword	Status	Notes
January	Monthly Newsletter for January	Newsletter	January 4th	December 28th		Complete	
	Inbound Content Marketing Article	Blog post	January 9th	December 28th	Inbound content marketing	Complete	Keyword: Inbound Content Marketing
	LinkedIn Post - Promote upcoming webinar	Linkedin post	Jouary 12th	January 12th		Complete	
	Webinar Appearence with ACEC	Webinar	January 18th	January 18th		Complete	101 Attendees, 7 new LinkedIn connections
	LinkedIn Post - Highlights of webinar	Webinar	January 19th	January 19th		Complete	
	Marketing in the Age of Artificial Intelligence	Blog post	January 23rd	January 23rd	Marketing and AI	Complete	
	LinkedIn Post - Video promotion of article		January 30th	January 31st		Complete	
February	Monthly Newsletter for February	Newsletter	February 1st	February 2nd		Complete	
	Website development cost article	Blog post	February 6th	February 8th	wesite development cost	Complete	Keyword: Website Development Cost
	Podcast Appearence - Marketing/AI	Podcast	February 8th	February 8th		Complete	Hosted by the Visible Expert Podcast
	Phography session with Kristin	Media kit	February 15th	-		In Progress	
	Webinar appearance with ACEC	Webinar	February 22nd	-		In Progress	
	How to lenghten articles blog post	Blog post	February 27th			Not Started	
March	Monthly Newsletter for March	Newsletter	March 1st	-		Not Started	
	March article	Blog Post	March 8th	-	Need new keyword	Not Started	Topic needed!
	Guest article for AAM	Guest blog	March 21st	-		Not Started	Topic: Inbound content marketing
	Webinar appearance with ACEC?	Webinar	TBD	-		Not Started	
	2nd March article	Blog Post	March 20th	-		Not Started	
	Emerge Conference	Speaking	March 24th	-		In Progress	Submit presentation by March 12th

FIGURE 5.2

What goes into a content calendar? Some experts create very detailed calendars and use them to track results over time. You may want to start simpler until you get the hang of it. At the very least, include the following five elements:

1. **Title.** Note the title of each presentation, blog post or guest article that you plan to write or deliver. When drafting titles, don't forget to include keywords when appropriate.
2. **Internal and external deadlines.** Note when the final product is due, as well as any interim deadlines for reviewing, editing and submitting the piece. Submitting materials when they are due is a great way to make editors and event organizers happy.
3. **Support resources.** Identify any individuals or functions whose help you need to bring the article or presentation to fruition. Examples include graphic designers, writers and editors.
4. **Status.** When you are managing multiple pieces of content, each of which is in a different stage of production, it's important to keep track of where you are. You might use language as simple as "in progress" and "complete." Or you might want to indicate where in the process each piece is (writing, editing, final proofreading, waiting for submission and so on). How you approach this column will depend on how many projects you are managing, how many people are involved and how complex your process is.

5. **Publish or presentation date.** Indicate when the piece was actually published or presented. This could be different from the due date, which can help you evaluate your performance over time.

In addition to the five elements above, you might want to include other features, as well. For instance, you might add a column to identify the type of content (blog post, guest post, LinkedIn post, webinar, speaking engagement, etc.) and another to capture any keywords that need to be included. In a larger organization, you might want to identify which expert will deliver each piece. And you might provide a notes column where you can document lessons learned, challenges, results and other details.

FAILING TO COMPLETE IMPORTANT ACTIVITIES IS OFTEN THE UNDERLYING REASON YOU DON'T ACHIEVE THE RESULTS YOU WANT.

Your content calendar is a great way to turn your visibility plan into a practical working document. It also allows you to track what you did and didn't accomplish. Failing to complete important activities is often the underlying reason you don't achieve the results you want. For this reason, your content calendar may be your best tool to provide personal accountability.

SEARCH ENGINE OPTIMIZATION (SEO)

Search engine optimization, or SEO for short, is the single most important technique an expert can use to be found in online search. SEO is a wide-ranging discipline, with many facets, subtleties and technical implications. And because Google changes its algorithm continually—often with little explanation of those changes—the field is always evolving. But the fundamentals of SEO rarely if ever change, and every Visible Expert needs at least a general understanding of how it works. Going a step further to learn the most basic skills—keyword research and page optimization—is not particularly difficult if you have the time and inclination. Whether you decide to dive in and master the more technical aspects of SEO, or work with an expert who handles them for you, is up to you.

Let's begin with a quick overview of how a search engine works.* Search engines regularly send out automated bots to track down every website they can find. These bots crawl through a website's pages and index anything that has changed since the last time they came to the site. Search engines use these indexes to try to understand what each page on a website is about. The search engine's algorithm then tries to determine which pages provide the most authoritative information on a topic, and it displays links to these pages in relative order of importance whenever someone conducts a search. The string of words a person types in Google when they conduct a search is called a keyword or keyword phrase (many people use these terms interchangeably).

How do you position your blog posts and online articles to rank high in Google's search engine results? There are four basic components to an effective search engine optimization campaign.

Site and page optimization. Site optimization involves making sure that your website is set up for success. Google not only needs to be able to crawl your entire website without running into barriers, it is also looking for pages that load quickly and deliver an excellent user experience on both desktop computers and mobile devices. Site optimization is highly technical and is best left to an experienced web developer. Page optimization, on the other hand, is the part of SEO that you as an expert have the most direct control over. It involves researching the best keywords for a page and incorporating them into your text. While we can't cover keyword research in this book, there are plenty of good tutorials online to get you started. Other signals that Google may use to determine if your page is high quality include using metadata—adding effective page titles, meta descriptions and alt text to the appropriate elements of each page—and whether you link to other relevant pages on and off your website.

---

* When we say search engines, we're talking primarily about Google, the runaway industry leader with over 90% of market share at the time of this writing.

Off-site SEO. Off-site SEO is a critical strategy you will use to convince search engines that your content is worth paying attention to. To oversimplify a bit, think of each link from somebody else's website to yours as a vote of confidence. The more links you have from high-quality third-party sites—especially sites that are themselves established authorities—the more Google is going to think your content is valuable. Getting these links back to your content (which, appropriately, are called "backlinks") is an art. As you become better known, these backlinks will pop up organically when people who know and respect you begin linking to your thought leadership from their own content. But at first, you will probably have to put in some work to get them. One of the most straightforward ways to get backlinks is to write guest blog posts that include a link or two back to content on your website.

Quality content. Another key to effective search engine optimization is producing quality content that answers the questions that searchers in your target audience are asking. As you select keywords and write your content you should always have this audience in mind. Does the keyword reflect actual user intent? Keywords can sometimes have multiple meanings. So before you write your next blog post, google your keyword and make sure the existing list of results matches your intended meaning. If not, you are probably going to have a tough time making it onto the first page of search results. Are your readers looking for a quick definition or examples? If so, consider incorporating those in your piece. You may even want to set these sections apart with clearly labeled subheads. Are you providing your own thinking on a topic? Or are you simply rehashing someone else's ideas? Do you explore a topic in more depth than the other pages you are competing against?

Content promotion. It's not always enough to create thoughtful, well-optimized online content. You've put a lot of effort into it, so you want to give your work the most visibility you can. That means actively promoting it. As soon as you publish a piece of content, share it on social media. If you have a PR resource, consider using them to spread the word. Set up your blog to allow subscribers, then automatically alert them when a new article is posted. You can even send out an email to your list with links to your latest and greatest stuff.

It's in search engines' best interest to deliver the most relevant and highest quality content to their audiences. If you work with them—following the latest SEO guidance and producing original, well-crafted content—even a solo practitioner can begin ranking well in search engines for relevant keywords. That's not to say it's easy. Most experts and firms will want to seek out a qualified SEO partner to help them on their journey. Look for one that not only knows SEO inside and out, but also understands the professional services. Selling professional services is very different from selling single-lens reflex cameras or vacation packages. And if a SEO practitioner promises a quick, inexpensive fix that seems too good to be true, it probably is.

DEVELOPING YOUR TOOLKIT

Putting together your toolkit can seem like a daunting task. And chances are, it will be if you try to do it all at once. Unless you have a big team to support you, a better approach may be to add tools over time. Start by looking at the communication channels you've chosen in your visibility plan and prioritize the tools you will need to use those techniques. In most cases, you will need most or all of the tools we described above. Some of these tools, such as your credentials package and media kit, can be developed in stages. Go ahead and put together the pieces that are practical now, then add the missing elements later on. When tackling the larger tools, such as your website and email marketing system, you may need to look outside for help.

When it comes to the website, some experts find themselves in a situation where they work for a large organization and they have little control over how the website is structured or how their bio is presented. In these cases, you may need to lean more heavily on your social media channels. They may give you more flexibility to tailor your profile. You may encounter a similar dilemma when dealing with a company-wide email marketing system. Here again, you may need to improvise if you are associated with an organization that limits your flexibility. Some experts rely on their personal email, sending individual messages rather than doing bulk mailings. Or if your firm allows it, you can use a third-party email marketing platform like MailChimp or ConvertKit to provide email delivery and automation functionality.* Alternatively, you could go all-in with LinkedIn, using its many features to build network connections and share content.

There is one strategy you might try to get around restrictions inherent in your organization. Ask your firm to set up a Visible Expert pilot program. This is exactly what Nishith Desai did with experts at his international law firm. Such a program may give you more flexibility and access to tools that are otherwise off-limits.

If you are an expert in solo practice or in a small organization, you may have more flexibility but fewer in-house resources to help you build the tools. In this situation, your best option may be to retain outside talent to develop the tools you can't handle internally, much as Dan Adams did. This kept Dan on track as his organization implemented different steps in their plan.

In the next chapter, we'll discuss how to carry out your plan, including how to track your performance and how to determine what impact your plan is having on your organization. We will also give you tips to troubleshoot performance problems and make adjustments during your Visible Expert journey.

---

* Every experts' needs are different, so we don't endorse any specific software platforms. We include these examples as a starting point to do your own research and find a solution that is right for you.

» Your **visibility toolkit** includes the critical infrastructure you'll need to support the implementation of your visibility plan. Most experts will need help to get everything set up and working smoothly.

» A **high-performance website** includes specific features. It will be the centerpiece of your program and the place where much of your content lives.

» Your **credential package, press kit and social media profiles** are important tools that make building your visibility easier. They contain information not usually found in a standard professional bio.

» An **email marketing system** gives you a way to communicate directly with your contacts and nurture the relationship over time.

» A **content calendar** is an essential tool to organize and track your content development activities.

» **Search engine optimization** is one of the best and most effective ways to be found online. If you will be writing a great deal of blog content, you will need to learn the basics of keyword research and page optimization. For technical SEO, choose a partner who understands the professional services.

CHAPTER SIX

IMPLEMENT
YOUR
PLAN

BEFORE WE EXPLORE HOW TO IMPLEMENT YOUR PLAN, LET'S PAUSE FOR A FEW MOMENTS TO APPRECIATE HOW FAR YOU HAVE COME. You have learned how to find a niche that addresses a significant challenge of your target audience while accommodating your personal strengths and preferences. You have determined what issues and topics to write and speak about and which channels are best to reach your audience. And you have considered how these channels will address your three major business development challenges. You have also planned out how often you will use those channels, which you have documented in a detailed content calendar. You've made huge progress! Now take a big breath. It's time to put your plan into action.

Today, it's easier than ever to raise your visibility. A technological revolution and dramatic changes in buyer behavior over the last decade have created new ways to reach your audience. The rise of internet search, people's expectation that most information is free and available instantly, and democratic new tools to discover and consume information have transformed the way professional services are bought and sold. At the same time, many of the traditional ways firms built their businesses are in decline. If current trends continue, for instance, online search will soon overtake referrals as the most common way buyers look for a professional services partner. And face-to-face networking may never completely return to its pre-pandemic levels.

What has been a considerable challenge for firms, however, has been a boon for individual experts. It is now relatively simple and inexpensive to make your expertise available to hundreds or thousands of people. And unlike traditional thought leadership, experts have myriad tools available to monitor metrics like engagement and conversion rates in real time.

In this chapter, we'll explore the details of implementing your plan and how to track your performance, troubleshoot problems, and learn from your experience. We will also look at some of the common challenges that experts face and how the Visible Experts we've met have overcome them in the real world.

Let's begin with the learning mindset you will need to get the most from your investment of time and energy.

THE LEARNING AND GROWTH SPIRAL

If you follow the roadmap we have laid out in this book, you will research your target audience and consider which strategies and tactics align with your goals and talents. Then, using the best information available to you, you will develop a visibility plan customized to attract your niche audience. But no matter how thoughtful and careful you are, you will get things wrong. As you gain experience and determine what does and doesn't work for you, you will need to adjust your plan. You will find that some tools and tactics are better suited to you than others.

You will also discover that your market evolves. For instance, new competitors may enter your space, or new communication channels may emerge, displacing old ones. Your clients' challenges and interests can change, too, so you may need to adjust your issues and topics over time. Think about this evolution as a learning and growth spiral (see Figure 6.1). If you commit to continuously learning and growing, you will find that you are often trying out new ideas. But before you invest heavily in a new tool or technique, it's important to test it first.

» The Learning and Growth Spiral

FIGURE 6.1

TEST
MEASURE
LEARN

Of course, you want to avoid tests that are not reversible. In other words, make small bets that you can abandon or undo if they don't pan out. Do you have a new marketing channel that you think will be productive? Test it on a limited scale and see what results you get. Don't go all in and commit to it in a way that is difficult or expensive to undo. Testing also involves measuring the impact of what you do. By measuring the impact of the test, you will learn what works and what doesn't work, what engages your audience and what generates no response. From that new learning comes new ideas, and yes, new tests, new measurements, and new learning. The concept itself is simple. Make small reversible bets, test them, measure the impact, and learn from each test. If you do this systematically over time, your approach will become more and more effective as you learn and grow.

Next, we turn our attention to how you should track the impacts of your visibility plan. In other words, what should you be measuring to help you see emerging problems and improve your success?

TRACKING PLAN IMPLEMENTATION

Let's start by tracking the implementation of your plan. Are you actually doing what you said you were going to do? It's hard to overestimate the importance of actually following your plan. The reason is simple. If you only partially or inconsistently implement your activities, you aren't going to achieve the results you expect. If you don't do it, it won't work. Tracking your activities keeps you accountable. If you work in a larger organization and you are trying to develop multiple Visible Experts, tracking each expert's progress is also a great way to introduce accountability into the equation.

There are generally two reasons that things go wrong. The first reason is that the technique never gets implemented at all. The second reason, which may be harder to recognize, is that the technique was executed incorrectly. It may have been implemented in a way that limited, or even worked against, success. Your content calendar is a good place to track your progress. As we mentioned in Chapter 5, your content calendar lays out what you are going to do and when you are going to do it. Simply add a column where you indicate whether you completed the activity at the scheduled time. This is also a great place to note anything you might want to change or test in the future.

There are several ways to bring accountability into this equation. One is to use a coach or consultant to keep you on track, troubleshoot problems and provide regular feedback. We do this at Hinge for many of our Visible Expert clients, and it keeps people motivated and moving toward their goal. A firm developing multiple Visible Experts might share each expert's progress in a staff meeting or other forum. Social pressure can be a powerful motivator. There is a variation on this theme for solo practitioners, too. Share your progress with a friend or colleague and ask for their perspective on your journey. We have talked to several Visible Experts who formed small groups to help each other grow and improve. We'll revisit this concept of experts helping experts in the next chapter.

> IF YOU DON'T DO IT, IT WON'T WORK.

When anyone reviews an expert's progress they should be asking two sets of questions: First, did you do it? Did you fully implement it as planned? Second, what did you learn? Was the communication well received? Was your audience engaged? Were there any measurable results? Have you learned anything that might make it more effective in the future? Here's where the learning and growth spiral really starts to have an impact. Small incremental improvements over time make a big difference.

Once you have a process in place to track the implementation of your plan, focus next on the impact that your activities are having on your audience.

TRACKING THE IMPACT ON YOUR AUDIENCE

Your Visible Expert plan is worthless if nobody pays attention. That's why it is important to keep an eye on the impact you are having on your audience. You can measure your impact in three ways. First is your visibility. Are more of the people you want to attract discovering you? Second is your expertise. Do your audiences know what you are an expert in? Third is list growth. Is your list of prospects—people you can communicate with directly—growing? Let's consider each of these in detail.

Tracking visibility. There are two easy ways to measure visibility. The first and perhaps single best indicator is your blog traffic. Each month, look at how many visits you are getting to the blog posts you have written. The more readers you have, the greater your visibility. Be sure to filter out traffic from inside your firm, particularly if you work at a large organization.

There should be more to your analysis than overall traffic, however. Take a look at other online metrics, such as where that traffic is coming from, which pages they are visiting, and how long they spend on your site. Figure 6.2 includes a list of web metrics you may want to monitor. Of special interest is traffic that comes from non-branded organic search—non-ad-driven traffic that comes from search terms that do not include your name or your firm's name. This will tell you how well your search engine optimization is performing. Over time, SEO should drive a considerable amount of traffic to your blog posts.

FIGURE 6.2

» Metrics to Track Your Visibility

WEBSITE METRICS	SOCIAL MEDIA METRICS	OTHER METRICS
Acquisition Metrics • Sessions • New Users • Total Users • Event Count **Engagement Metrics** • Pageviews • Bounce Rate • Active Users • Engagement Rate • Average Engagement Time • Conversions	**Awareness** • Impressions • Number of Followers **Engagement** • Likes • Comments • Shares, Retweets, etc. • Mentions • Click-Through Rate	• List Growth (Number of Mailable Contacts) • Downloads of Premium Content • Number of Speaking Engagements

Your social media traffic and followers (see Figure 6.2) are other components of your visibility. These are particularly important if social media plays a significant role in your visibility plan. Some organizations develop an index that looks at a combination of specific website traffic and social media activity. This gives them a single visibility number to focus on.

Tracking expertise indicators. Expertise indicators include any downloads of premium content pieces that demonstrate your expertise, such as executive guides, white papers, research reports, ebooks or webinars. Tracking these indicators gives you a measure of how deeply your audience is engaging with you. In addition to downloads, consider tracking visits to content-rich sections of your website such as your blog or content library. Once again, if you like to keep things simple, you could create an expertise index by combining your premium content downloads and blog visits.

Tracking list growth. Your contact list is a critical component of your visibility plan—and bigger is better. That means you will want to monitor its growth. Each contact on your list is someone with whom you can communicate directly, either through email or on a social media channel (if email is not possible in your situation). The larger the list the more people you can convert into new business opportunities. The number to track for your email list is the number of mailable contacts—that is, people who have not unsubscribed or generated a hard bounce. This is a standard metric included in every email platform. On the social media side, you'll want to track the number of your LinkedIn connections. On other platforms, you can keep an eye on your followers. Once again, if you use multiple platforms, you can total up your connections and followers to create an index of your total reachable audience.

TRACKING BUSINESS RESULTS

While it's important to track your activities and how they are being received by your audience, what you are ultimately trying to produce is business results. When we say business results, we're talking about more than just revenue. A lot has to happen before a new client closes. There are several indicators that affect your business profitability and growth. Let's look at some of the more common business indicators that every Visible Expert should track.

Leads. Leads are people who want to learn more about you or your services. Some may even be ready to have a conversation with you. If these people meet certain criteria (such as minimum budget, project size or schedule), they are generally referred to as qualified leads. Your overall leads and qualified leads are indicators of whether your plan is having the desired impact.

Opportunities. Opportunities are fully qualified leads that have actively engaged with you and are likely to want a proposal. A single client or prospect may represent multiple opportunities. Of course, not all opportunities result in proposals.

Proposals. These are the proposals that you deliver to opportunities. Most experts track both the total number of proposals and their dollar value. Some also track the types of services offered in the proposals.

Wins and losses. What portion of the proposals turned into new work? What proportion were unsuccessful? For what type of clients and for which services? This analysis helps you determine the effectiveness of your third challenge, closing the sale.

Financial impact. Consider the financial parameters of the work that you win. This includes revenue, profitability, and any other economic indicators that tell you how successful your engagements are.

» Metrics to Track Your Business Results

TOP OF FUNNEL	BOTTOM OF FUNNEL	FINANCIAL IMPACT
• All Leads • Qualified Leads • Opportunities	• Total Number of Proposals Sent • Proposals Won/Lost • Win Rate • Total Value of Proposals Sent • Total Value of Proposals Won • Average Time to Close • Services Sold	• Total Revenue • Profitability • Average Lifetime Value of a Client • Rate of Repeat Business

By tracking measures of your visibility, expertise, list growth and business results, you equip yourself with data to troubleshoot problems and unfulfilled expectations. And of course, troubleshooting is the first step toward improving performance.

We will get to troubleshooting in a moment. But first, let's return to one of our experts and see how regular monitoring and troubleshooting impacted his visibility plan. Dan Adams' firm targets large, sophisticated organizations, so getting their marketing right is a high priority today. But that wasn't always the case. As Dan admits, "before we started our visibility journey we weren't really tracking the performance of our website. Now we have professional help. We meet every month. We review what's happening on our website and how it's going." To capture the data they need, Dan's firm relies on software. "Using HubSpot and other tools we're able to track our online performance and how many downloads we are getting. We put some of our content behind a registration form, so we know which companies are coming to us and what their interest level is. All this has made our marketing more professional."

As important as tracking is, automating the follow-up process produces a much better and more consistent user experience. "When somebody downloads one of our resources—say a whitepaper—they will get three automated emails spaced a few days apart. And if it's a very attractive looking prospect (because again, we focus on large companies), we'll send a personal email to that person and try to reach out to them directly." The results? Dan's firm has seen a five-fold increase in web traffic and a significant financial impact. Tracking and troubleshooting make a difference.

TROUBLESHOOTING POOR PERFORMANCE

For over 15 years, we have studied the performance of professional services firms. This research clearly shows that organizations that track marketing performance and adjust their strategy and tactics accordingly are more profitable and grow faster. So the case for tracking and making adjustments is clear and compelling.*

When you track your implementation, visibility, audience response and business results you have everything you need to troubleshoot performance issues. These insights will help you determine where you are falling short and where you need to improve. If you find yourself underperforming in a particular area, ask yourself these five questions:

---

* To see the data for yourself, check out Hinge's High Growth Study: www.hingemarketing.com/highgrowth

1. **Am I doing what I said I was going to do?** This is a question that speaks directly to implementation. Did you actually do the activity you said you were going to do when you said you were going to do it?

2. **Am I targeting the right audience?** Do you have clear evidence that you have reached the right audience, or have you inadvertently targeted a different audience? To find out, take a good look at who is responding to your content and promotions and try to determine whether they are in your target audience. Keep in mind that you will always attract some unqualified outliers, so focus on the majority of the group.

3. **Am I doing it frequently enough and devoting enough effort?** You may be doing what you say you're going to do, but you aren't giving it sufficient attention to be successful. For instance, producing two podcast episodes a year is unlikely to move the needle.

4. **Do I understand how to do it correctly?** Are you implementing the communication technique correctly? Suppose you take a few minutes each day to share your content on social media but you rarely respond to questions or comment on other people's posts. This is like attending a networking event and only talking about yourself. Doing the activity the right way makes all the difference.

5. **Is my message and content differentiated and relevant?** Look critically at your content and think about whether it addresses your audience's business priorities. Are you saying anything insightful or thought provoking? Or are you just regurgitating well-worn industry best practices? If you aren't producing new insights or demonstrating superior expertise, your content is likely to fall short of your goals.

If you find this sort of troubleshooting difficult, you may want to consider getting outside help until you develop the skills and confidence to do it yourself. A coach or team who understands how to implement these strategies correctly can often dramatically accelerate your progress.

OVERCOMING PERSONAL CHALLENGES

What do you do if you run into problems as you troubleshoot your program? In this section, we address some of Visible Experts' most common and vexing challenges. We also describe real-world strategies other experts have used to address them. Sometimes these solutions involve a new technique or a hidden shortcut. Other times they require a simple shift in perspective or an adjustment in priorities. Remember, whatever challenge you encounter, others have faced it, too—and found a way past. So let's see what we can learn from them.

NOT RECOGNIZING THE IMPORTANCE OF VISIBILITY

The Challenge. It's easy to put off starting your Visible Expert journey, especially when things seem to be going well. This is the dilemma that Dan Adams faced. "When we started our business, I focused on doing the work, but I didn't focus on the visibility part at all. I just wasn't paying attention to that. Business was going well. I was enjoying what I was doing. We were helping clients. And most people had never heard of me."

How They Solved It. Often the solution to this dilemma is to change how you think about your responsibilities. That was the case with Dan Adams. "Recognizing that part of my job was to be visible was extremely important. Some of the things we've done over the last few years have dramatically elevated that visibility. We still do the same things we were doing before, but now it's a lot more fun."

This is an extremely common situation in our work with Visible Experts. Almost to a person, they wish that they had started their Visible Expert journey earlier. As Dan puts it, "Replaying it again, I would've advanced my pursuit of visibility by many, many years."

OVERCOMING THE IMPOSTER SYNDROME

The Challenge. Impostor syndrome is a common psychological phenomenon where people doubt their own skills, expertise and accomplishments. These doubts are often accompanied by a fear that they will be exposed as a fraud and not a real expert deserving of the status they have attained.

It's easy to start assuming that you don't deserve to be recognized as an expert. Rachel Fisch, an expert in accounting technologies, describes her experience: "I think any Visible Expert probably goes through a phase of what they call imposter syndrome. I found it so odd that people would know my face and my name at events where I didn't know anybody. You say to yourself, I can't possibly be the one that these people are looking to for expertise."

How They Solved It. Overcoming imposter syndrome typically involves changing your mindset or perspective. Rachel recognized the syndrome for what it is and used it as motivation to always be prepared. "I think it's okay to have those thoughts and to work through them. In my case, working through them means just digging in deeper and working harder—making sure that I know the situation with my clients. That I'm positive, I've done the research and I do not feel uncomfortable."

This approach works for Rachel because it fits her personality. "For me, probably because of my introversion, I need to feel comfortable and really confident before I start talking to others about a topic. So that means that if you've got Rachel speaking at an event, I know what I'm talking about."

But other experts may require different shifts in their mindset. Michael Zipursky, a Visible Expert who is focused on helping consulting firms, explains: "Early on, my biggest challenge was to step up and get my ideas into the marketplace. But like many experts who haven't done that before, I questioned myself: Are my ideas good enough? Are they original enough? Are they going to be valuable enough? At some point, a switch flicked and I realized that I had to get past this being about me and make it about the people I wanted to serve. How could I create more value for them? That meant giving them more content, insights and data—helping them learn from my experiences and accelerating their success."

PRODUCING CONSISTENT, HIGH-QUALITY CONTENT OVER TIME

The Challenge. Michael Zipursky knows this challenge well. "You don't get to a place where you're called a Visible Expert if you're not consistent. You don't write just one article or give one talk and then, suddenly, people consider you an expert. Usually, there's a whole body of work—and a great deal of time and thought and effort that has been put into it. So, to me, that's a big one." It is a big one indeed.

How They Solved It. Michael explains how he and his team tackled this daunting challenge. "We overcame the barrier of being able to put out these ideas consistently in two parts. The first was making sure that we had the right systems in place: how we go about developing content or doing our own research studies. The second part was making sure that I got team members involved. No longer was it okay to have Michael, head down, cranking out an article. Rather it was, let's think about who on the team can send out a survey to a segment of our list to get some initial information to help us to validate our hypotheses. And who else can help us take the outline or ideas that I've created and draft an article. So the team is doing the bulk of the work, and then I will jump in later and edit it or add some new ideas or stories. That's true whether it is an article or a presentation that I'm giving."

It's important to remember that getting outside assistance with your content is not just for large organizations. As Jody Padar explains, "I'm a CPA by trade. I'm a good writer, but I'm not an editor. One thing that set me apart was that my blogs were always well written because I wrote them, and then they were professionally edited so they were always ready for publication." As Jody soon realized, this extra step gave her a competitive edge. "The people who accepted my blogs loved to have me because I was giving them a polished piece. That wasn't always the case with other professionals." The lesson here is to find a way to shore up your weaknesses so you can focus on higher-value activities.

GENERATING MORE MEASURABLE IMPACT

The Challenge. What do you do if you are not seeing the business results that you were expecting? Usually, this is a sign that some part of your business development process is not performing as it should. Until you can determine where your process is falling short, success will be elusive. Use the Troubleshooting section above to try to determine what you need to fix.

How They Solved It. Dan Adams explains his business' journey to high performance. "Today, we see performance increase a lot. But it didn't happen until we had a new website in place and started promoting content." Dan hired an outside organization (the authors' firm, Hinge) to help troubleshoot their marketing program. Once they had identified their biggest problem areas, they set to work solving them. Before long, they started to see positive results. Dan explains what they believe is happening in the marketplace that drives these results. "Before, if people heard our name and checked out our old website, they might just keep looking for somebody else. But now they see a well-crafted website, case stories and a lot of useful content, and they go, 'Oh, okay. Maybe this guy is someone we want to hire.'"

Dan cautions that even if you have the key tools in place, visibility won't necessarily come right away. "It's not the sort of thing that's going to happen overnight. We don't care about that, but we do like the trajectory. We're seeing that people in the industry are talking about us. It's very, very powerful when people hear about you from more than one source—and that some of the sources are other people. That helps a lot." That is the power of a strong Visible Expert brand. Just keep in mind that it takes patience and the willingness to solve problems along the way.

IF WE DEVELOP VISIBLE EXPERTS ON OUR STAFF, WON'T THEY JUST LEAVE?

The Challenge. In the last few years, there has been a lot of staff turnover and talent shortages in the professional services, so this is an understandable management concern. Are you going to invest a lot in your people just to watch them walk out the door?

How They Solved It. The solution is not to avoid making your experts visible. Instead, make your organization more resilient so that resignations become almost irrelevant. According to Nishith Desai, the Visible Expert who built an entire law firm of Visible Experts, "Resignations should not make organizations vulnerable. So how do you do that?" Here is his formula:

"Number one, you continuously create leaders, and nurture leadership traits." Give people the training and opportunity to exercise leadership so they can develop their leadership skills. "Number two, train, educate and upskill your people." Here he is referring to giving your people the technical and subject matter skills to broaden and deepen their technical expertise. But leadership and technical skills are not enough. "Number three, it is very important to make them visible. Sometimes a leader or a senior person trains people very well. But if he or she leaves, there is a vacuum because the client has no connection with the more junior people, and junior people do not have visibility to the client. That causes gaps. To fill the gaps, it is important that when leaders are training and upskilling they also make their junior leaders visible." As it turns out, the secret to making your organization more resilient is not to limit the development of Visible Experts, but to accelerate it. Having more Visible Experts in your organization reduces risk. In fact, Nishith Desai has made developing Visible Experts part of his firm's growth strategy.

> HAVING MORE VISIBLE EXPERTS IN YOUR ORGANIZATION REDUCES RISK.

Today, retaining top talent can be difficult. But it would be a mistake to assume that your Visible Experts will leave. In fact, many will reward the opportunity you gave them with loyalty. Others understand that finding another firm that will support their visibility with the same enthusiasm won't be easy. And if one of your experts rises to Visible Expert Level 5 and leaves to start their own business, at least your firm will always be part of their success story, making you even more attractive to top young talent.

MANAGING A HYPER-COMPETITIVE ENVIRONMENT

The Challenge. Competition can be brutal. Many Visible Experts have a network of fellow experts they can tap for support and encouragement, but that's not always the case. Jody Padar, author of *The Radical CPA,* describes the competition she encountered when trying to partner with CPA industry software vendors. "When you are working at this level, there's only so much money that goes to influencers at the top. It's a limited budget. As you start to climb, you forget there are other consultants that may not want you to be there—because these software vendors only have limited resources that they spend on consultants or influencers to the profession. And now you've just encroached on their pot of money. I was young and dumb. I just thought, 'Oh, this is the best thing ever. My ideas are about making the world a better place. Everybody's going to love my ideas, and I'm going to share them. And it's all going to be warm and fuzzy.'"

How They Solved It. This is a very good reason to do competitive research, as we described in Chapter 3. You don't want to be surprised by direct or indirect competitors. Jody goes on to explain how she had to adjust her understanding of the marketplace of ideas: "I realized that there were people out there who would push me down because I was a threat to their income and power. And when I started to really see how things really were, I thought, 'Wow, it really is a business. And there are people who will try and stop you. There will be people who will take your ideas and claim them as their own.'"

Jody reevaluated how she treated her intellectual property. She began to publish her original ideas so the world would know they were hers. "When you're starting a movement, you want people to take those ideas and spread them because that's what makes the movement move. Yet it is also a business, and you must think about what's your IP, and what's not."

SHOULD YOU CHARGE FOR YOUR CONTENT OR GIVE IT AWAY?

The Challenge. Should you charge for your content or give it away for free? That was the dilemma that confronted Jody Padar. "I was giving away my content, giving away my speaking, giving away so much because it was really part of this greater movement." Jody realizes that there is a distinct benefit associated with making your content free and easily accessible. "Because I gave it away, it allowed me to build my visibility. If you look at people who start charging for their content right away, nobody buys their stuff. People think, 'Oh, you're fly-by-night. You're just selling something.'"

How They Solved It. Many Visible Experts offer a mix of free and paid content. Early on, as you are establishing your reputation, you'll want to minimize friction. Free is the way to go. But later, as you become better known, you may be able to increase the perceived value of your content by charging for some of it. "For four or five years, everything that I did was a labor of love," says Jody, "not because I was expecting to get paid for it, or wanted to get paid for it, or even knew I could get paid for it." With time and experience she learned that people *would* pay for her thought leadership, and she struck a balance that suited her and her audience.

What's going to be the right approach for you? If your expertise is focused primarily on a cause such as social change, you may want to prioritize visibility over revenue. Carl Elefante, the architect who focuses on sustainability in the built environment, is a good example. At this stage of his career his priority is to get his message out as broadly as possible, so he makes his content freely accessible to all. That doesn't mean that *everything* he does is free, however. For example, the book he is writing will be offered for sale.

Kimberly Ellison-Taylor is a good example of a Visible Expert with multiple priorities. On one hand is her professional focus on technology and accounting, which has clear financial goals. On the other hand is her passion for diversity, equity and inclusion. In this arena, she prioritizes spreading her message broadly over generating income.

If your area of expertise is squarely in the commercial realm, you may want to begin by making all your content free, then as your visibility increases you can gradually introduce paid options. It is rare for an expert to charge for all of their content, however. It's hard to build visibility if you don't offer at least some of your material for free. If you put your most valuable content behind a registration form (still free!), you can begin collecting contact information from your most interested followers. That establishes a direct communication channel (usually email) and sets the stage for potential paid engagements in the future. Just keep in mind that anything you put behind a registration form is invisible to Google and will not show up in search results.

THE NEED TO EVOLVE YOUR EXPERTISE

The Challenge. You work in a dynamic marketplace. Technology, buyer behavior, buyers' needs and the competitive environment are always evolving. As experts, we need to keep up with all that change. Mark Amtower, who markets to the federal government, says it well. "The visibility factor brings a lot of things to you, but it also brings a lot of responsibility. If you're a Visible Expert, it becomes incumbent upon you to make sure you're at or near that cutting edge of your discipline."

How They Solved It. The solution, of course, is to evolve your expertise. Mark describes his evolution. "As a marketing guy, my area of expertise has evolved with the market. In the '80s, I was the king of direct marketing because I would go into federal mailrooms to see how mail was received and distributed internally. I'd look to see what got tossed and why. In the '90s when Netscape and email were becoming popular, I had to adapt. Direct mail was going away, and that was fine. You have to adapt. By the early 2000s, we had all these Web 2.0 Tools. So, I had to adapt again. When social networks came in, I had my biggest leap of all."

Jody Padar loves to evolve and wears her brand, The Radical CPA, with pride. "I've always been radical. I've always had thoughts that were kind of outside the norm." Jody's embrace of everything new suits her well and is reflected in how she positions herself as an expert. "What's cool about The Radical CPA brand is that it evolves as I evolve," she says. "Back in the day, it was cloud, new tech, new processes, new pricing and the new CPA firm model. But moving forward, it moves into artificial intelligence and machine learning and whatever's next. What's cool about The Radical CPA is it's always radical. It's always growing and it's always changing."

OVERCOMING THE NEED FOR PERFECTION

The Challenge. No one wants to make a fool of themselves. That's why many experts invest a great deal of time and energy preparing their thought leadership materials and making sure that they are flawless. Unfortunately, perfection isn't possible, especially when you are working at the forefront of your area of expertise. So how do you avoid the paralysis of endless refinement?

How They Solved It. Michael Zipursky solved this problem by changing his mindset. "My big belief is that the greatest results come from taking imperfect action. It's never about waiting for things to be just right or the perfect time, because rarely does that exist. It's about putting your ideas out there and being prolific with them. And understanding that to get to a great idea, you usually have to have a lot of bad ideas. But if you stop because you're concerned about putting out a bad idea, you're never going to get to that great idea."

KEEPING TRACK OF YOUR COMMITMENTS

The Challenge. Most Visible Experts have busy lives with many commitments and deadlines. How do you keep track of all of these activities without dropping a ball?

How They Solved It. Kimberly Ellison-Taylor is an expert in technology, so you might expect her to use something very sophisticated. You'd be wrong. Instead, she likes to keep things simple. "Yes, I like checklists. Maybe that's the accountant in me. But every day, I want to have a list of things that I want to work on. And I need reminders so that I don't forget the most important ones."

That's it. There are a lot of options out there to keep track of your life, from powerful, feature-rich apps that let you run your day like a project manager to ye olde pen and paper. But as you weigh your options, Kimberly has two pieces of advice. First, "it is important to not have a complex system." Second, find a tool "that allows you to collaborate across several different devices."

IMPLEMENT YOUR PLAN

Once you've created your visibility plan it's time to put it into action. Remember the learning and growth spiral? No plan is perfect, and yours won't be either. Accept it. Embrace it. As long as you measure what you're doing, track the results and learn along the way you can perfect your plan on the go. And when you want to try something new, add it to your plan. Just make sure that you're making small reversible bets in case it doesn't work out.

As you implement your plan, record your progress in your content calendar. Be honest with yourself—or ask someone to monitor your progress for you. If you don't get to something, or take an activity half-way, record that, too. This is the best way to keep yourself accountable and moving forward. Remember, sticking to your plan is what is going to bring you the visibility you want. Don't be the person with a great plan that was never put into action.

Track your plan's impact on your audience in three important areas. First, how is your plan affecting your visibility? Are you seeing growth in your website traffic and social media followers? Second, look at your expertise indicators. Are your web visitors downloading your expert content? Are they visiting sections of your website, such as your blog (and most importantly, the blog posts you wrote), that demonstrate your expertise? Third, monitor your list growth. Is your mailable email list growing? How about your social media followers?

Next, look at your business results. Are you generating new leads? Are these leads turning into opportunities and proposals? Are you winning proposals at a rate that meets your business goals?

Revisit these metrics on a regular basis—at least monthly. At the end of each business quarter you may want to do a more in-depth analysis in which you focus on long-term trends and performance. Ask yourself the troubleshooting questions in this chapter to determine if you need to make adjustments to your plan.

Finally, as you uncover potential issues, read over the challenges and potential solutions that we describe earlier in this chapter. They may provide the guidance or insight you need to get back on track.

TAKEAWAYS »

» Implementing your visibility plan is an ongoing process of testing, measuring results and gaining new insights.

» To monitor your performance, you should track three key areas: how well you are implementing your plan, its impact on your audience and your business results.

» If you discover problems along the way, use the troubleshooting guidance in this chapter to determine what's gone wrong.

» Real-world Visible Experts have had many of the same problems you will encounter. You may be able to use the lessons they learned to overcome your own difficulties.

» CHAPTER SEVEN

SHARPEN YOUR EXPERTISE

MOST VISIBLE EXPERTS DEVELOP THEIR INTEREST IN A PARTICULAR AREA EARLY IN THEIR CAREER. IT'S ONLY LATER THAT THEY COMMIT TO NARROWING THEIR FOCUS AND RAISING THEIR VISIBILITY. In this final chapter, we turn our attention to the important process of sharpening and maintaining your expertise. You will learn that most experts use multiple techniques to keep their skill set well honed. In many ways, it is an organic process that builds on your personal learning style.

Kimberly Ellison-Taylor exemplifies this approach. "I'm doing formal learning and informal learning," she says. "I'm in classrooms. I'm talking to other Visible Experts. I'm looking at YouTube videos. I'm looking at LinkedIn Live broadcasts. The learning never stops." While this may sound intimidating at first, it can also be exhilarating and rewarding. Continuous learning requires a certain amount of dedication, but it doesn't have to be overwhelming. We're going to explore a variety of techniques that will make it easier to keep your expertise in peak shape. Let's begin by looking at how other experts sharpen their expertise.

Figure 7.1 shows the top methods that experts use to hone their technical expertise. These methods span everything from reading to conducting research to taking the time to think. A number of experts also note the importance of approaching this task with the right mindset. Let's start there.

FIGURE 7.1

» Top Methods Visible Experts Use to Keep Their Expertise Sharp

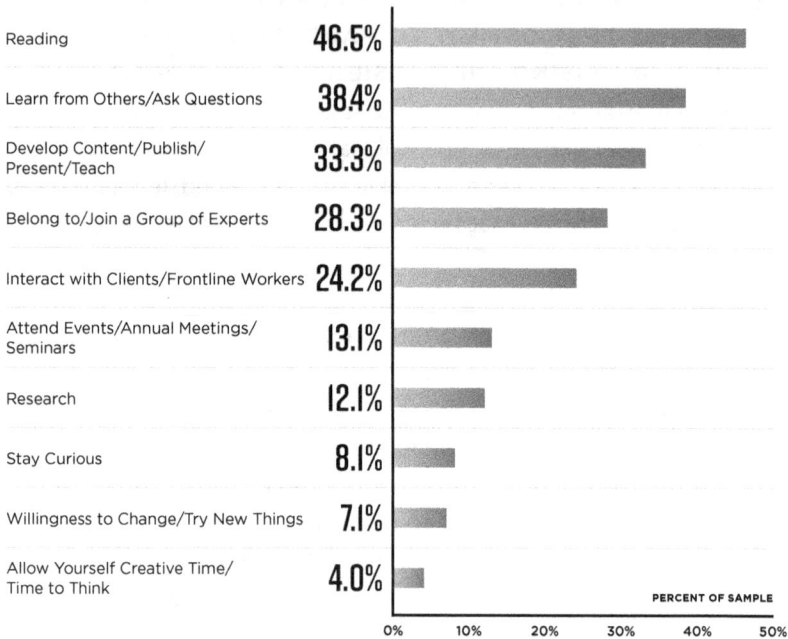

Method	Percent
Reading	46.5%
Learn from Others/Ask Questions	38.4%
Develop Content/Publish/Present/Teach	33.3%
Belong to/Join a Group of Experts	28.3%
Interact with Clients/Frontline Workers	24.2%
Attend Events/Annual Meetings/Seminars	13.1%
Research	12.1%
Stay Curious	8.1%
Willingness to Change/Try New Things	7.1%
Allow Yourself Creative Time/Time to Think	4.0%

PERCENT OF SAMPLE

0%   10%   20%   30%   40%   50%

DEVELOP A CONTINUOUS LEARNING HABIT

In the last chapter, we introduced the concept of the learning and growth spiral. We described it in the context of incrementally improving the execution of your visibility plan. But it applies just as well to the process of growing your expertise.

As an expert, you are constantly learning new things, trying them out and adding them to your basket of skills. Some things you try will fail. But often, we learn the most from our mistakes. A defining trait of all Visible Experts is that they have learned how to learn. They've learned how to look for new ideas and integrate them into what they already know. They've learned to question their own assumptions and beliefs. They've learned to be flexible.

"I've learned how to learn," says Kimberly Ellison-Taylor. "And in learning how to learn, I can learn anything." She goes on to explain the importance of learning from all your experiences. "I make it a practice to try to learn something in every environment. And that means looking for connections that also strengthen and expand my own thinking."

But as important as a continuous learning habit is, don't put unrealistic expectations on yourself. "I don't feel like I must know every single detail," says Kimberly, "even in the areas I'm an expert in. Because in the next 20 minutes, it's already changed. It may be that you know who knows it and you know where you can get it." Sometimes it's enough to know where you can find an answer when you need it.

Kimberly is making another important point, too. It's perfectly acceptable to ponder a tough question before you answer. Give yourself the time and space to get the answer right rather than feel pushed to answer on the spot. "When someone asks a tough question," says Kimberly, "I want to give them a specific answer, so I give myself the time to really think it through. And people appreciate that."

LEARN TO LOVE QUESTIONS... AND QUESTION EVERYTHING

Almost every Visible Expert we know appreciates questions. Questions from their audience, from their clients and even from other experts. Why? Because the questions people ask help us understand how well we are communicating our ideas, what problems our audiences are concerned about and what emerging issues we need to start thinking about in earnest.

Sometimes questions can raise legitimate doubts about our current knowledge. Rhondalynn Korolak describes how people's questions have forced her to pause, reflect and change course. "They caused me to rethink things and unlearn things, which is tough. Unlearning is actually the toughest part of maintaining your status as an expert. We need to constantly unlearn things that are now no longer correct to stay sharp and to stay at the leading edge of what we're doing. Because as things change, and as we become aware of new information, we may realize the way we've always done it is wrong. And to really be solid experts, we must always be open to that."

Being open to change is important if you want to remain relevant and credible in an evolving world. Next, let's explore strategies you can use to maintain your edge.

COLLABORATING TO LEARN

Collaborating with other experts is a powerful way to keep your expertise and skills razor sharp. Accounting expert Rachel Fisch would agree: "Other experts are critical to building a community that can challenge each other, that can feed off each other, that can collaborate and innovate with each other. I think the expression is 'steel sharpens steel.' It offers a unique opportunity that is not easy to find anywhere else."

There are at least two types of collaboration: formal and informal.

Formal collaboration often involves a structured process to solve a specific problem or develop a new set of regulations or guidelines. This process is typically run through a trade association, university, government agency, think tank or similar organization. In this situation, the sponsoring organization brings a group of experts together at a specific time to produce a specific result.

Remember Nishith Desai, the Mumbai-based attorney who built an international law firm of Visible Experts? Because they have so many experts, covering so many areas of innovation, they have become a go-to resource for government agencies, trade associations and international regulatory bodies when it comes to developing new regulations or policies. They have helped craft policies in emerging areas as diverse as cryptocurrency, medical devices, international dispute resolution, educational technology and drones.

These formal collaborations can result in new industry guidelines or government regulations. And the individuals involved in the expert panel benefit from their heightened visibility and prestige, as well as their intimate knowledge of the new rules. Who better to help you with a policy or regulatory issue than an expert who helped create it?

But formal collaboration can take different forms, too. For instance, a group of like-minded experts may come together to help each other grow and improve their practice. They might set up a formal mentoring program or develop a marketing partnership where multiple experts collaborate to develop a book, a webinar or a conference. In architecture, urban planning, industrial design and similar industries, experts convene in intensive sessions called design charrettes to solve a complex problem in a short amount of time.

> A DEFINING TRAIT OF ALL VISIBLE EXPERTS IS THAT THEY HAVE LEARNED HOW TO LEARN.

There are many variations on this theme. Let's explore a few examples of strategies used by some of the real-world Visible Experts you've already met.

Rachel Fisch found her collaborative community online. "Accounting Salon is my place to go when I need to talk to other experts who know what it's like to speak at conferences and what it's like to be a Visible Expert. Reaching out to that community is really critical to my own well-being, as well as to my Visible Expertise." These interactions have many benefits. "I've also had the opportunity to learn from some of the best minds in the accounting industry within these expert communities," says Rachel. "And what's really interesting is how generous we all are with our time and knowledge. It's almost like there is a humility that comes with fantastic expertise."

Mark Amtower has a very different formal approach. He mentors a small number of professionals. While they may not yet be very visible, "My mentees are experts," says Mark. "As a rule, I don't adopt people who are early in their career. I'll answer their questions, but I'm not going to adopt them into my mentee circle because these are people I work with at least once a week. My mentees are usually at a senior marketing, director or CMO level. So they're bright, and their feedback is worth tons. Don't tell them", he adds with a wink, "but I get as much guidance from them as I give. And whether or not they understand it, their questions and insights push me in new directions."

EXPERTS NEED OTHER EXPERTS.

Mark also collaborates with other Visible Experts to produce high value thought leadership. Michael Lisagor, another federal marketing expert, approached Mark with an idea to write a book together based on blog articles that they had published in the past. The result is the excellent new book, *How to Win in the Government Market: Hundreds of useful tips from two of the most experienced GovCon experts.*

So why are high-status experts so willing to collaborate and share their expertise? We posed this question to Jody Padar. "I'm part of a networking group that's all Visible Experts. When you attain that status there are very few people who do what we do. Where else are you going to learn best practices without figuring it out yourself and making a bunch of mistakes?" Experts need other experts. They have a mutual respect because they understand what it takes to become a Visible Expert. "As you rise in the ranks," explains Jody, "you're now part of that 'club.' Now people are more willing to share with you because they feel 'Okay, you've made it to this level. You did the hard work to get here. Now that you're here, we'll share with each other because it's going to be helpful to all of us.'"

Informal collaboration. Collaboration, of course, doesn't have to be pre-arranged. Informal collaboration can also be a powerful tool to learn and grow. For many experts, this happens at conferences and events or among friends and colleagues.

Rachel Fisch attends conferences not only to learn from other presenters, but to interact with her target audiences, potential vendors and business partners. "When it comes to accounting conferences, I not only attend them as a speaker, but I try to get to as many sessions as possible. I not only learn about the content that's being taught, but I'm also learning what the rest of the audience is learning. I'm learning what's resonating with them, and what their questions are on that topic. I'm learning the style of the presenter, I'm learning PowerPoint tips and what I might want to do in my next presentation." But her learning doesn't stop there. "It's also a great opportunity to spend some time with the vendors, to not only talk about their typical sales pitch to accounting firms, but also to spend some time going into the problems my clients may have. I explore the potential for strategic partnerships for myself and my clients. So, there're a lot of ways you can get information out of a conference besides just speaking and attending."

Mark Amtower takes another approach to informal collaboration. "It's impossible to be a Visible Expert—a thought leader—without input from people who are at the same level. You must get feedback from these people. Finding experts out there who are willing to brainstorm and share with you, as long as you're open in return, that's the coolest thing about being a Visible Expert."

WRITING TO LEARN

Writing is one one of the best ways to learn. That's important because if you are like most Visible Experts, writing is a major part of your visibility plan. As you recall, an important trait of a Visible Expert is their ability to explain complex issues in simple, easy-to-understand language. Writing forces you to think this way: to organize your thoughts, construct clear, coherent arguments and address any gaps in your knowledge. To fill the gaps, you can do the research yourself or reach out to the appropriate expert for answers. This kind of writing—the kind that pushes the frontiers of your knowledge, builds your expertise muscles and keeps you intellectually fit—is also the kind of writing that attracts the most attention and elevates your reputation. We talked to some of our Visible Experts about the role writing played in their professional lives.

Jody Padar didn't start out as The Radical CPA. Back then "most people thought that I was nuts," she quips. But the interesting thing about her evolution as a thought leader is the critical role her writing—and the feedback it generated—played in clarifying and focusing her expertise. Her story begins relatively early in her career. "I had recently joined my dad, who had a traditional accounting firm focused on tax work with individuals. He told me to develop my own clients. It was a blank slate because the prior firms that I had worked in were more established. I realized that I would have to do things differently. And it was really confusing to me."

Writing was a way for Jody to work through the issues, get feedback and crystalize her thinking. "I started to write, and those writings became blog posts, which became content for Twitter, which allowed me to share things more frequently. I was really evolving my thoughts about my practice as I was implementing them. That became my thought leadership base."

Some of her ideas about technology reshaping the accounting profession seemed strange to many of her professional peers. "The things I was talking about were so newfangled that most professionals couldn't even wrap their minds around them. They thought that I was wrong and that all the things that I was talking about aren't going to be relevant. What happened is that I started to find people who believed in what I believed in. These were other CPAs and other tax professionals. You start with a small group of followers, and they start to engage with you, and they believe in you, and it spreads." This core audience expanded as her early ideas were validated and became a blueprint for a successful modern accounting practice. Jody went on to write her groundbreaking book, *The Radical CPA*, which soon became her expert moniker.

In fact, writing a book can be the tipping point for many experts. When Rhondalynn Korolak wrote her second book, it helped her develop her revolutionary way of thinking about cash flow. "I highly advocate writing books. For me, writing a book has two benefits: One, you get your message out. Two, you codify what you think you know." This is a powerful combination. A book can dramatically increase your visibility and credibility, as we discussed in Chapter 4. And because a book requires you to delve deeply into your topic, the process of structuring, researching and writing is almost guaranteed to sharpen your expertise. "A book is a place where you can assimilate all your knowledge," adds Rhondalynn. "You have to put things down in a way that you can communicate them to anybody. As you write, you start to formulate new systems and processes."

Most experts would agree. According to our research, writing a book is a top technique for increasing an expert's visibility. As you may recall, Dan Adams' book helped establish his credibility and build trust. But you don't necessarily need to write a full-length business book to reap at least some of these benefits. Many blogs and other publications are looking for thought-provoking, shorter pieces. Kimberly Ellison-Taylor writes prolifically on a wide range of issues. "I love to write. What I really appreciate today, is that they don't want a novel. They want about 600 words. I can easily do 600 words. I think it's really important to have written pieces of various lengths because there are people who appreciate reading something quickly, getting the gist, and then moving on."

What short pieces lack in depth they can make up for in clarity and incisiveness. They still compel you to do your research, organize your thoughts and produce valid conclusions. If you can't explain complex concepts simply, in a few words, you probably don't fully understand it.

TEACHING TO LEARN

Teaching is a natural extension of Visible Expertise. Like writing, it forces you to organize your thinking and explain complex concepts simply and clearly. But it's also a two-way street. Your learners may ask questions that uncover gaps in your knowledge or point to possible new directions for your own learning. Teaching is also a great way to increase your visibility. It plays a central role in many of the techniques experts use to extend their reach and engage new audiences. Any time you conduct a webinar, run a workshop, participate in a podcast or speak at a conference, you are teaching.

Teaching to learn fits many Visible Experts' personalities. As we explained in Chapter 1, a willingness to share their expertise is a characteristic of many successful Visible Experts. This was the case with Michael Zipursky. "Growing up, I thought I wanted to be a professional athlete. At the end of high school and into early university, I had already started a business and my mind was all about being an entrepreneur. But my mother, grandmother and several teachers said to me, 'You would be a really good teacher.' I thought they were crazy. I didn't want to go into academics. I wanted to build things and grow. But as time went on, I recognized that where I get the greatest fulfillment and enjoyment is from helping others, whether that's working directly with clients, delivering a webinar or doing a workshop."

Doing work every day that fulfills you is a fantastic motivator— and a wonderful benefit of Visible Expertise. But it is not the only benefit of teaching. "In order to teach," says Michael, "you need to really understand the topic. Otherwise, your students or clients will see through it. For me to deliver a keynote talk or a webinar— or even create new training for our clients—requires a strong understanding of what I'm going to share. That process of teaching helps me stay sharp."

It's also an easy way to figure out what's working and what isn't. "One of the great benefits of working with clients or a group of people," explains Michael, "is that you can get feedback very quickly about what resonates, what doesn't, how things can be improved and what people see as valuable. That process provides a very quick feedback cycle, which also helps me to stay sharp."

Dan Adams certainly agrees with this point. In engagements with product development organizations, he and his team deliver a lot of workshops. "We have the opportunity in workshops to sit with our clients for days at a time," says Dan. "And there is so much we can learn from them. We can tell when something we say clicks with them. We can observe what they're not getting quickly, too. We kind of feel their pain. During the workshops and in follow-up web conferences, we pay a lot of attention to what they're struggling with and what they need. That keeps us at the forefront of our subject matter."

> RESEARCH IS A GREAT WAY TO SHARPEN YOUR EXPERTISE AND SPREAD IT TO THE WORLD.

RESEARCHING TO LEARN

There are plenty of good reasons for Visible Experts to love research. As we explained earlier in this book, research reports are one of the most valued types of content. For instance, executives are eager to learn what their competitors are thinking about and prioritizing (we humans love to compare ourselves to others). They will gladly fill out a form—and sometimes pay a lot of money—to get a fresh piece of research that gives them insight into their marketplace. Research is also a great opportunity to learn and raise your expertise game. Whenever you conduct research, you get access to brand new information that is available to no one else, and because you immerse yourself so deeply in the data, you often glean more from the findings than someone who simply reads your report.

Research can come from sources within your firm (informal research) and other organizations (secondary research). Or it can be an original study that you conduct or commission yourself (primary research). In all cases, you can use the insights to improve your skills, spot new trends and identify promising new opportunities. Research is a great way to sharpen your expertise and spread it to the world.

Many experts start with reading. We're not talking about consuming other firms' content or reading for pleasure. Instead, we mean diving deeply into your subject matter. Often this involves looking outside your industry for insights and inspiration. For instance, you might follow Visible Experts outside your core profession to find new ways to think about your own area of expertise.

"I read a lot," says Jody Padar. "I probably consume as much content as I produce. I keep a broad perspective and look toward what's next because that's who I am. If it's content marketing, chances are it's not what I'm reading. I'm reading evolving stuff that isn't mainstream yet."

At Nishith Desai Associates (NDA), each attorney focuses on a specific trend or emerging issue. "We look at research reports done by McKinsey, Boston Consulting, or other leading consulting firms to learn what trends they are seeing," says Nishith Desai." We follow them because all the consulting firms generally rely on primary research, which is their forte." Instead of trying to compete with these consulting firms, they collaborate with and learn from them. "Our forte is not number crunching. What we do is pick up trends from them, apply our own logic and select which trends we want to take a bet on. Then we start visualizing and talking with other experts— 'What will be the strategic, legal, tax or ethical problems that will be coming up in the next four, five or ten years?' We start working on approaches and possible solutions now. This allows us enough time to prepare ourselves, so when the actual time comes we are ready to help our clients while our competitors are struggling to understand the issues." Of course, the experts at NDA don't just research these emerging issues. They are writing and teaching about them as well. They are increasing their visibility as they hone their expertise.

Many Visible Experts also do primary research on their target audiences. This research often involves surveys or interviews of their target audience. Because primary research provides answers to the questions you want to answer, it can be invaluable in elevating your expertise. We discussed this process extensively in Chapter 3.

Dan Adams and his firm, The AIM Institute, conduct primary research and use it not only as a powerful marketing tool but as a way to strengthen their expertise, as well. For example, in a recent study on the drivers of B2B growth, Dan and his team surveyed over 500 executives and identified 24 growth factors. They were able to apply much of what they learned—insights available to nobody else in the industry—to their own practice.

SHARPENING YOUR EXPERTISE

You can't be a true Visible Expert unless you really are an expert. There's no faking it. And because your profession, technology and marketplace are continually evolving, there is no true, final destination. Instead, expertise is a long but inspiring trek up the mountainside. You may pause from time to time to catch your breath and admire the spectacular views, but the peak is always over the next hill. Visible Experts like you never stop learning and improving. It's the nature of your work. And you learn to love the challenge.

In this chapter, we described the many different ways you can sharpen your expertise as you wend your way to greater and greater visibility. Identify which approaches are the best fit for your personal style and preferences. Then review your visibility plan again. What activities have you already built into your plan? If you will be writing or teaching, you've got baked-in opportunities to grow as you expand your reputation. When you're writing a blog post, take the time to do some research and update your understanding of the topic. When you're conducting a webinar, pay close attention to the questions people ask and think about what you can learn from them.

And ask yourself questions, too. Are you keeping up with emerging trends? Is your thought leadership still insightful, or are you just rehashing the same old material? Are you lagging behind, or do other experts look to you for new ideas and leadership?

To make progress you can't always fall back on what you know and what is easy. From time to time, you have to push yourself and engage your sense of curiosity. As you prepare your thought leadership materials—and as you embark on this incredible, exciting journey—don't be afraid to tackle some of the tough questions. Always be on the lookout for those gaps in your knowledge that require a little more research or a little creative thinking to build a bridge and inspire your audience. This is how you achieve enduring expertise.

» You can't be a Visible Expert unless you have significant expertise in something. So you must keep your expertise sharp and relevant.

» Develop a continuous learning habit. You will always be testing, measuring and learning. The learning never stops.

» Collaborating, especially with other experts, is one of the best ways to hone your expertise. Other Visible Experts have experience and perspectives that are hard to find elsewhere. Most Visible Experts are generous and freely share their expertise with other experts.

» Writing is an important way to keep your expertise sharp. It forces you to organize your thoughts, express them clearly and identify areas where you need to improve.

» Teaching also forces you to think clearly and sharpen your skills. One of its big benefits is immediate audience feedback, which you can use to improve and grow.

» Research is an excellent way to take your expertise to a new level. This may involve doing informal research, using secondary research from a third party, or conducting primary research on your target audience.

WHERE TO LEARN MORE

WE KEPT THIS BOOK SHORT SO THAT EVEN BUSY PROFESSIONALS COULD READ IT IN A FEW SITTINGS AND VISUALIZE THE EXCITING PATH THAT LIES AHEAD. But to achieve Visible Expertise requires applying skills and tools that may be new to most experts. We couldn't possibly cover these in sufficient depth without adding hundreds of pages. Even if we had tried, technology changes all the time, and this book would be out of date as soon as it was released. Fortunately, there are many excellent resources available online, in other books and elsewhere that can teach you these skills—from researching keywords to producing a webinar to using social media to promote your content.

If you want a one-stop shop, Hinge University is an online learning platform designed specifically for professionals like you and your team. Learn new marketing skills or brush the rust off those you haven't used in a while. And for those who are visual learners, we have created a four-and-a-half-hour companion online course that walks you through creating your Visible Expert plan from start to finish. It includes interviews with all of the experts featured in this book, as well as a detailed workbook you can use to create your plan as you work through the course. For firms that want to elevate a team of experts, Hinge's Visible Expert Enterprise Program leads them through the process and provides ongoing mentoring and implementation support. To learn more about these resources, download templates and access other valuable materials, visit **hingemarketing.com/revolution**

Most of the experts you met in these pages learned these skills on their own as they developed their practices. You can do it, too! Just take it slow, and don't try to tackle more than one or two new activities at a time. Remember, you have a powerful advantage those experts didn't—a proven program that will allow you to sidestep traps and mistakes that would have slowed you down or stopped you in your tracks. Equipped with the strategies in this book, you can build your visibility faster and with less frustration than you could have ever imagined.

Are you ready to take your career through a revolution?

ACKNOWLEDGEMENTS

WRITING A BOOK LIKE THIS IS NOT A SOLITARY ACT. The act of putting the words down on a computer was just one process in a larger, complex operation. In fact, the authors could never have produced this volume without the enthusiastic support of a band of co-conspirators.

We tip our hats first to all the experts who participated in our studies. While only a handful made it into the pages of this book, every one of them was essential to improving our understanding of how a Visible Expert is made. Each had the courage and resilience to overcome self-doubt and adversity to build a reputation of astonishing power. And they generously shared their stories, advice and insights with us so that others might follow their lead. They are inspirations to the rest of us.

Drafting a book is one thing. Getting the manuscript in shape for publication is quite another. To our editor and business partner, **Aaron Taylor**, we express our sincerest gratitude for turning our drafts into polished, easy-to-read prose. In many places, he contributed new ideas or reworked existing ones to make the narrative more clear, complete and engaging. We also would like to appreciate the proofreading talents of **Kelly MicKey**, who combed through the manuscript and plucked out numerous errors and inconsistencies.

A heartfelt thank you to **Candace Frederiksen**, who managed the Visible Expert interviews and who conducted all of them herself. She has a gift for connecting with people, and she made the experience easy and pleasant for our experts.

This book wouldn't have been possible without the research that underlies it. **Ethan Keyserling**, our Director of Research, was essential to every aspect of our latest study—from designing the questionnaire to coding the responses and conducting the analysis. The full study of 220 Visible Experts and 275 of their clients is available for download from the Hinge Research Institute.

Christian Baldo designed the cover and interior layout of this book. His enormous talents have made the final product not only impeccably professional but a lot more fun to read. **Kristin Claeys**, another wonderful and talented designer, also contributed in many important ways to the quality and polish of the finished product.

We would also like to thank all those who work tirelessly to spread the word about this project, especially **Rowena Figueroa, Kevin Bloom** and **Kelly MicKey**. They know as well as anyone that writing and publishing a book is only the beginning.

Finally, we would like to applaud **Austin McNair** for wrangling all of these disparate people and herding them toward a common goal. Without his project management skills and unflagging cheerfulness, this book would still be a work in progress today.